RETIRED
GREYHOUNDS

A Guide to Care and Understanding

This lovely greyhound bitch shows what beautiful dogs greyhounds are.

RETIRED GREYHOUNDS

A Guide to Care and Understanding

Carol Baby

Foreword by Jilly Cooper

THE CROWOOD PRESS

First published in 2010 by
The Crowood Press Ltd
Ramsbury, Marlborough
Wiltshire SN8 2HR

enquiries@crowood.com

www.crowood.com

This impression 2021

© Carol Baby 2010

British Library Cataloguing-in-Publication Data
A catalogue record for this book is available from the British
Library.

ISBN 978 1 84797 165 4

Illustrations by Charlotte Kelly, based on original artwork
by the author.

Photographs by Liz Rodgers unless otherwise credited.

Typeset by Jean Cussons Typesetting, Diss, Norfolk
Printed and bound in India by Replika Press Pvt Ltd

CONTENTS

ACKNOWLEDGEMENTS

My thanks to Liz Rodgers who worked tirelessly with me on the photographs, and Nick Guise-Smith for donating racing photos so that all proceeds from the book could go to Greyhound Rescue West of England.

Thank you also to Carol Forde and Barry King for advising on Chapter 2, and to the Somerset homing team from Greyhound Rescue West of England, and Anne Pullen, for support and proof reading. Thank you to Sandra Morris for inspiring me to learn about how dogs think and communicate, to Kay Andrews and Ann Morgan, and my husband Bob, for believing in me.

FOREWORD BY JILLY COOPER

My greyhound, Feather, who came to us through GRWE, had a terrible start in life. In the middle of winter he was turned out in a muzzle on a motorway in Ireland. Unable to eat, drink or fend off other dogs, it was three weeks before he was found. Somebody had also tried to burn the racing tattoos off his ears. But despite this dreadful experience, he has proved the most lovely, affectionate, charming, biddable, kind dog we have ever owned, who also keeps us in fits of laughter.

Many greyhounds have appalling lives once their racing life is over, or when they are no longer any use for breeding. Some of them are just chucked out, like Feather, or receive a bullet through the head or end up in desperately over-

Jilly Cooper with GRWE dog Heather.
(Photo by Simon Bird)

crowded kennels or, worst of all, are sold to run their hearts and bodies out for incredibly cruel trainers on tracks abroad.

All this should never happen, because greyhounds make the most wonderful pets. Some of them obviously need training when they come to their new owners straight off the racetrack.

In this lovely book, the very knowledgeable Carol Baby will take you on a most rewarding journey. She will tell you how to find the right dog; how to introduce it to the strangeness of domestic life, how to house train it; teach it to play and have fun; teach it to get on with other dogs and cats and to give infinite pleasure to children. Few dogs are more charming with children than a greyhound. Feather always causes shrieks of

joy from my grandchildren, when he takes off and races round and round the field or big lawn just for the fun of it.

Greyhounds are equally miraculous with older people. My husband Leo, who has Parkinsons, is unsteady on his legs. Feather never pulls on the lead and slides past him like a skein of silk – but admittedly steals his reclining invalid chair at every opportunity!

This is a lovely book. Carol Baby does not pull any punches that anyone rescuing a greyhound will need time, patience and above all love, but it is a worthwhile adventure and I am convinced if you follow Carol's guidance you will end up with a glorious dog.

Jilly Cooper, 2010

OPPOSITE: *The author with her lurcher, Ash, and ex-racing greyhound Foxy.*

1 THE GREYHOUND BREED

BREED DESCRIPTION AND CHARACTERISTICS

There is no doubt in greyhound lovers' eyes that they are the most beautiful dogs, long-legged, streamlined and elegant, sleek and dignified – but the beauty is not just skin deep. Greyhounds are gentle and affectionate, quiet and loyal, calm and loving. It is a pleasure and a privilege to have one living in your home.

The fifteenth-century Boke (book) of St Albans characterized the greyhound as 'headed like a snake, neckewd like a drake, backed like a bream, tailed like a rat, footed like a cat'. This makes the breed sound like bits and pieces of different animals put together without thought, but a greyhound is far better designed than that. However, the quote does tell us that people were writing 'breed standards' for ancient breeds such as greyhounds as far back as the fifteenth century!

Beauty in greyhounds is not just skin deep: kindness shines out of those eyes.

Racing greyhounds are bred purely for their ability to race and win, rather than for looks. This is what keeps the breed healthy, as dogs with inbred defects are unlikely to be winners. Well bred racing greyhound pups will be sold for between £3,000 to £10,000, and an already proven dog will sell for upwards of £20,000; the price tag therefore acts as an incentive to make sure that no inherited defects are apparent in racing greyhound stock. So when you take on an ex-racing greyhound it is unlikely to have any predisposed inherent defects, and it will have a long pedigree, including winners. Racing greyhounds tend to be smaller than show greyhounds, and are not bred to Kennel Club requirements. However, I have included the Kennel Club breed standard, as it is interesting to compare your ex-racing greyhound and see how it matches up.

THE KENNEL CLUB BREED STANDARD

A Breed Standard is the guideline which describes the ideal characteristics, temperament and appearance of a breed and ensures that the breed is fit for function. Absolute soundness is essential. Breeders and judges should at all times be careful to avoid obvious conditions or exaggerations which would be detrimental in any way to the health, welfare or soundness of this breed. From time to time certain conditions or exaggerations may be considered to have the potential to affect dogs in some breeds adversely, and judges and breeders are requested to refer to the Kennel Club website for details of any such current issues. If a feature or quality is desirable it should only be present in the right measure.

General Appearance
Strongly built, upstanding, of generous proportions, muscular power and symmetrical formation, with long head and neck, clean well laid shoulders, deep chest, capacious body, slightly arched loin, powerful quarters, sound legs and feet, and a suppleness of limb, which emphasize in a marked degree its distinctive type and quality.

Characteristics
Possessing remarkable stamina and endurance.

Temperament
Intelligent, gentle, affectionate and even-tempered.

Head and Skull
Long, moderate width, flat skull, slight stop. Jaws powerful and well chiselled.

Eyes
Bright, intelligent, oval and obliquely set. Preferably dark.

Ears
Small, rose-shape, of fine texture.

Mouth
Jaws strong with a perfect, regular and complete scissor bite, i.e. the upper teeth closely overlapping lower teeth and set square to the jaws.

Neck
Long and muscular, elegantly arched, well let into shoulders.

Forequarters
Shoulders oblique, well set back, muscular without being loaded, narrow and cleanly defined at top. Forelegs, long and straight, bone of good substance and quality. Elbows free and well set under shoulders. Pasterns of moderate length, slightly sprung. Elbows, pasterns and toes inclining neither in nor out.

Body
Chest deep and capacious, providing adequate heart room. Ribs deep, well sprung and carried well back. Flanks well cut up. Back rather long, broad and square. Loins powerful, slightly arched.

Hindquarters
Thighs and second thighs wide and muscular, showing great propelling power. Stifles well bent. Hocks well let down, inclining neither in nor out. Body and hindquarters, features of ample proportions and well coupled, enabling adequate ground to be covered when standing.

Feet
Moderate length, with compact, well knuckled toes and strong pads.

Tail
Long, set on rather low, strong at root, tapering to point, carried low, slightly curved.

Gait/Movement
Straight, low reaching, free stride enabling the ground to be covered at great speed. Hindlegs coming well under body giving great propulsion.

Coat
Fine and close.

Colour
Black, white, red, blue, fawn, fallow, brindle or any of these colours broken with white.

Size
Ideal height: dogs: 71–76 cms (28–30 ins); bitches: 69–71 cms (27–28 ins).

Faults
Any departure from the foregoing points should be considered a fault and the seriousness with which the fault should be regarded should be in exact proportion to its degree and its effect upon the health and welfare of the dog.

An ex-racing greyhound is like a retired Olympic athlete: remember what it is you have on the end of that lead! (photo provided by Nick Guise-Smith www.mirrorboxstudios.co.uk)

A greyhound is often referred to as a 'sight hound' or a 'gaze hound', which means that it uses sight more than its other senses to detect prey. Greyhounds have very keen sight and often spot prey long before we do. Other breeds that are classified as sight or gaze hounds include whippets, Salukis, borzois and Afghans, but the greyhound is the fastest of them all. The only animal faster than a greyhound is a cheetah. So when you take a retired greyhound into your home you have the privilege of taking in the equivalent of an Olympic athlete. You will be surprised how calm and docile they are in the house – but when you take them out, remember what it is you have on the end of that lead!

BREED HISTORY

The greyhound is one of the most ancient breeds of dog, produced by man's selective breeding for hunting animals such as the hare and the gazelle. Bones and teeth from archaeological sites and pictures painted on ancient pottery, pillars and tablets from Middle Eastern countries indicate that greyhound-type dogs were common there at least three thousand years ago, some say as far back as seven thousand. Similar dogs appear in artwork across Europe from medieval times. And yet the breed remains robust, sharing common ancestry with Arabian dogs such as the Saluki, the Pharaoh hound and the Slughi.

As the Roman Empire spread across Europe the greyhound came too, reaching England in the sixth century. Rich and poor families would have had such dogs to help provide food for the pot. Then in 1014 – during King Canute's reign – a law was produced that 'No meane man may own a Griehound', a sentiment many of us agree with, although the word 'mean' in this case actually means 'poor'. (It strikes me that Canute knew more about dogs that he did about the sea!) Only noblemen were then allowed to own greyhounds, which shows how highly prized they were (it is sad that in this and the last century that has not always been the case). This eventually led to the change in emphasis from hunting with greyhounds for food to hunting for entertainment.

In the sixteenth century coursing rules were drawn up by the Duke of Norfolk. In the eighteenth century greyhound racing meets became popular for greyhound owners, and they are still popular to this day, reaching their highest popularity in the years just after World War II.

SAINT GUINEFORT

There are many wonderful European legends about hounds' deeds and bravery. Gelert's story inspired many of us as children, and his grave can be seen at Beddgelert in Snowdonia, Wales. The story relates that Gelert was a wolfhound rather than a greyhound, but there is a surprisingly similar story of a greyhound called Guinefort, a thirteenth-century French tale in which Guinefort came to be regarded by the local people as a saint.

As in most of these legends, Guinefort's owner, a French knight who lived in a castle near Lyons, went out leaving his faithful greyhound to guard the baby. While he was gone a venomous snake came into the solar and slithered on to the baby's crib. Guinefort leapt into action, attacking the snake. In the mêlée the crib was knocked over and the baby landed safely underneath, while Guinefort killed the snake.

When the knight returned he saw the upturned crib and the dog with blood on its lips, but he did not see the baby hidden under the crib. He immediately jumped to the conclusion that Guinefort had killed the baby, and in fury drew his sword and killed his dog. Then he heard the baby cry and found the body of the snake, and realized what an awful deed he had done.

Filled with remorse and gratitude the knight and his family took the body of the dog to a disused well by the forest and placed it in there. They covered it over with stones and planted trees round it, making it into a shrine. The local people came to regard Guinefort as a saint for the protection of children, a belief which continued right up until the early twentieth century, and they would bring children to his shrine to be healed. The Catholic church never recognized him as a saint, however, maintaining that no dog could possibly be a saint.

Many of these legends abound, and they are all startlingly similar. It is difficult to know whether there is any truth in them, or whether they were cautionary tales (the moral being, 'Don't jump to conclusions until you have found out the whole story'). You can visit Gelert's grave at Beddgelert in Wales, which lends some truth to the story, but the gravestone is obviously more recent than mediaeval times. Sadly during World War II Guinefort's shrine fell into disrepair, and is now lost deep in the woods somewhere in France. Maybe I will go and find it one day.

Nevertheless, the fact that all these stories were about faithful hounds helps us to realize how loved and revered these dogs were so long ago, and it confirms our knowledge that these are wonderful dogs with a superb temperament, and which deserve the very best that life alongside humans can give them.

THE ORIGIN OF THE BREED NAME

Different reasons are given for the origin of the name 'greyhound'. Some say that all the early ones were grey and the colour variations developed later. It is interesting that Belayev, a Russian geneticist in the last century, experimented with breeding silver foxes selectively to improve tameness and ease of handling. These foxes were being bred for their pelts on fur farms, but were very difficult to handle. Over only eighteen generations, as the temperament improved, all sorts of colour variations mysteriously appeared in the breed. Did something like this happen to our greyhounds?

Another theory is that the word 'grey' is derived from the Latin word gradus meaning 'grade'. Dr Caius, the eminent sixteenth-century Cambridge physician, wrote:

> The greyhound hath his name of this word gre; which word soundeth gradus in Latin, in Englishe degree, because among all dogges these are the most principall, occupying the Chiefest place, and being simply and absolutely the best of the gentle kinde of houndes.

'Simply the best' – I'll go along with that idea!

Bo Jangles, Liz the photographer's dog, a really handsome greyhound – 'Simply the Best'.

2 THE BACKGROUND TO A RACING GREYHOUND'S LIFE

GREYHOUND WELFARE

The conditions under which a greyhound is produced can vary hugely from being born and kept alone in a cold, cheerless shed in someone's back garden, through to a state-of-the-art racing kennel with underfloor heating, double glazing and every conceivable luxury a racing dog might need. The biggest training yards can have from sixty to a hundred dogs at any one time. Most owners and trainers want the best for their dogs and take huge pride in breeding them and keeping them in tiptop condition ready to win. But, as in all sports, there are the rogues who will cut corners, save money, and who have little real affection for the dogs except as money-makers. These people have given the sport a bad name.

In May 2002 the 'Charter for the Racing Greyhound' was produced in response to a debate on the sport in the House of Lords in the previous year. A sixteen-point plan was produced by the Greyhound Forum, which was made up of

Some racing greyhounds are kept in cold, cheerless sheds in the trainer's back garden...

...while more fortunate ones live in state-of-the-art kennels with heating and double glazing.

greyhound's death: this should be done humanely by a veterinary surgeon, and only when destruction is inevitable.

It also discourages the over-production of greyhounds through indiscriminate breeding, although this is such a vague requirement that there is no way to enforce it; indeed there have been many cases highlighted recently of wholesale slaughter, where some layman has illegally shot unwanted dogs and buried them in his back yard.

It is a good charter and a real step in the right direction, but how do you quantify its success? And how do you enforce it?

A greyhound bitch will produce a litter of around six to ten puppies, but only

Greyhound pups are just as curious and mischievous as pups of any other breed.

representatives from various animal welfare charities together with the British National Racing Board (now called the Greyhound Board of Great Britain) and various racing bodies. It has helped to make a start in improving the life of greyhounds during and after racing – but there is still a long way to go. It covers the basic requirements of a living animal, which should hardly need to be spelled out in the twenty-first century, and offers recommendations as to the manner of a

THE GREYHOUND CHARTER

1. The registered owner and/or keeper of a greyhound should take full responsibility for the physical and mental well-being of the greyhound and should do so with full regard to the dog's future welfare.

2. All greyhounds should be permanently identified, properly registered, and relevant records kept by owner and/or keeper.

3. All greyhounds should be fully vaccinated by a veterinary surgeon and provided with a current certificate of vaccination.

4. All greyhounds must be provided with suitable food and accommodation and have unrestricted access to fresh clean water.

5. Adequate arrangements must be made to allow for exercise and socialisation.

6. Breeding and rearing – the over-production of greyhounds through indiscriminate breeding – must be avoided. Where a racing greyhound is bred from, the long-term welfare of the bitch and puppies must be paramount.

7. Training must be conducted so as to safeguard the long-term welfare of the dog.

8. Where destruction is inevitable, greyhounds should be euthanased humanely by the intravenous injection of a suitable drug administered under the supervision of a veterinary surgeon.

9. When transported, all greyhounds should be maintained in safety and comfort.

10. All tracks should appoint a member of staff responsible for animal welfare.

11. A supervising veterinary surgeon must be present whenever greyhounds are raced at tracks.

12. Tracks and kennels must be designed and maintained to ensure the highest welfare standards for the racing greyhounds.

13. Greyhounds must only race if passed fit by a veterinary surgeon immediately prior to racing.

14. Greyhounds must be entitled to receive emergency veterinary care if injured.

15. Drugs which may affect the performance of a greyhound when racing should not be permitted.

16. The industry must endeavour to ensure that all race courses have in operation a properly funded home-finding scheme for retired greyhounds. Such schemes should work closely with other welfare and charitable bodies seeking to find good homes for ex-racing greyhounds.

(This charter is credited to the Greyhound Forum and must be read in conjunction with the code of practice available from the Defra web site www.defra.gov.uk/corporate/consult/greyhound welfare/index.htm).

---

about 60 per cent of them will make it into racing. Those that are not going to make the grade are usually handed to rescue charities or are euthanased before they are a year old. Those that enter the charities as pups are good ones to choose if you have a cat, as they are usually young enough to learn to live safely and happily with it.

The pups will grow up in their family unit, which means they do learn to socialize, but as they will live only with greyhounds throughout their racing life they can find it difficult to socialize with other breeds of dog at first, and have little experience of the world outside their limited environment.

A beautiful greyhound bitch with her litter of puppies.

EARLY TRAINING

The age that greyhounds begin their training is around fifteen months old for a bitch and seventeen months old for a dog. If the young dog is very big this may be delayed for a few months to avoid putting excess strain on its limbs. The dog's keeper will have been watching its response to chase situations as it grows up, and will have a good idea of how keen it is going to be. By this time pups that show no interest at all in the chase will have been weeded out.

The dogs are taught to walk calmly on the lead without pulling. Lead-walking is a major part of their training regime, and in a large kennels one person may be walking two or three dogs at once. Given a racing weight of around 28kg to 36kg (62lb to 79lb) for each dog, and you can see why it is important that they walk well on the lead.

The young dogs will be put through a fitness programme that generally takes about six weeks. A local trainer's regime (borrowing terms from the horse world) goes something like this: first they will walk a mile every day for ten days, then go on to two miles a day for ten days. Then they will move on to trotting these distances – often the trainer will use a

Greyhounds are trained to walk well on the lead without pulling so that a number of dogs can be exercised at once.

A seventeen-month-old greyhound is introduced to the traps for the first time at the trainer's kennels.

As the trap opens he steps tentatively out...

... catches sight of the home-made lure being pulled swiftly ahead of him...

...and then he is off...

The excitement builds up as he chases the lure, gathering speed as he goes.

After successfully chasing the lure the greyhound is rewarded by being thrown a soft toy to play with. In his excitement he will probably rip it up.

bike to ride alongside them. When they can trot a mile without panting they will move on to full gallop, often using a track to run on and a man-made lure to chase. The training lure is usually made of a sack tied to a cable, on a reel. Just lying on the ground this would have no real appeal for the dog: it is the fact that it moves that makes it alluring, which shows you how strong the chase instinct is in these dogs.

It is against the law for trainers to use live bait to lure the dog. When the dog has chased the lure the trainer may throw it a soft toy to play with as a reward. This is why greyhounds often love soft toys.

During this time an owner will have been found for the dog. Anyone can own a racing greyhound, and anyone can apply for a training licence. Owners come from all walks of life, and sometimes own a dog in a syndicate. Generally owners are professional gamblers, farmers, businessmen and country people. Just as in the horse-racing industry, most dogs will live with the trainer and only see the owner occasionally. The dog will be given an identity tattoo in one ear (England) or in both (Ireland) so that it can be registered in the greyhound stud book.

The greyhound is given an identity tattoo so that it can be registered in the greyhound stud book.

RACING AND RACE TRACKS

Once the young dog is ready for racing a decision is made about where to race it. There are two types of track: registered and unregistered. Registered tracks are registered with the Greyhound Board of Great Britain (until January 2009 the National Greyhound Racing Board). These tracks follow the Greyhound Charter as closely as possible. On these tracks there are always vets in attendance, there is drug testing, and the welfare of the dogs is of paramount importance.

The unregistered tracks are known as flapping tracks, and at these tracks no drug testing is required, there does not need to be a vet in attendance, and in fact anything goes. Needless to say these flapping tracks are not popular with the animal welfare groups.

Registered Tracks
At a registered track any dog that is going to run in graded races must complete three trials: one on the empty race track, and two with two other dogs over the distance they intend to race. These trials usually take place in the early

ABOVE: Before any greyhound can race on a registered track it must complete time trials to assess its capability.

BELOW: The dogs come out of the traps at speed, knowing that the lure will be there for them to chase. (Photo provided by Nick Guise-Smith www.mirrorboxstudios.co.uk)

ABOVE: Greyhounds running a middle-distance race. (Photo provided by Nick Guise-Smith www.mirrorbox studios.co.uk)

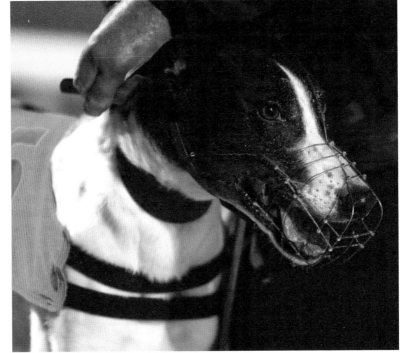

RIGHT: The vet checks that each dog is fit to race before it comes out on to the track. (Photo provided by Nick Guise-Smith www.mirrorbox studios.co.uk)

evening before the racing programme starts. The starting traps (like starting stalls in horse racing) and a mechanical hare are used, just as in a normal race, and the trials will be watched by a grader, who is probably the most influential person at the race track.

The grader must decide the sort of race the dog will be raced in, and which trap it should start in: if it tends to run wide round the outer side of the track it needs to start in an outer trap, and if it chooses to run close to the inside of the track it should start in an inner trap. Organizing the race so that each dog runs from a trap that suits its natural inclination helps to avoid collisions happening, as the dogs then tend not to cross in front of each other to run in their favourite place.

There are four different distances over which greyhounds race: sprint – about 250m (270yd); middle distance – about 450m (490yd); long distance – about 640m (700yd); and marathon – about 840m (920yd). As you can see, the measurements are not accurate because tracks vary, but all tracks have four bends so the races are usually referred to by the number of bends in the race. Thus a sprint is two bends, a middle distance is four bends, a long distance is six bends and a marathon is eight bends (or twice round the track). Just as all athletes, some dogs are better at short distances and some at longer ones.

Within the distances given above, races are graded from A9 (or sometimes lower, for example A13, depending on the track) to A1, with A1 being for the fastest dogs. Dogs gradually move up through the grades. Thus if a dog wins a race it automatically goes up a grade, and so the best dogs make it to the top, racing in A1 races. Some dogs get to their best grade and progress no further; also if a dog goes through a bad spell it may be moved down a grade. This way, dogs of similar ability are raced against each other, and all the dogs in the race have a fair chance of being placed in the top three. If a dog has been off work with illness, or has been injured or has suffered a racing fall, it must go through trials again to make sure it is fit before it can race. Many dogs spend their entire racing life racing on one track. Only dogs that achieve A1 status can travel around the country entering Open races at other tracks.

Greyhounds generally race once a week. When they arrive at the track they are checked by the vet, and then placed in a secure kennel away from the public.

Dogs often get bumped and fall at the first bend where they are still bunched together. This is where severe injuries can happen. (Photo provided by Nick Guise-Smith www.mirrorbox studios.co.uk)

The kennel is locked and no one is allowed access unless the trainer is present. This is to prevent dogs being 'nobbled' or interfered with in any way. The dog must stay there until its race, when its trainer will come to collect it to put it in the trap.

The first bend in the race is where there is the greatest likelihood of dogs bumping each other and of falls happening, so someone is always on duty there to help any dog that is injured. By the time they get to later bends they are not so bunched up so there is less likelihood of falls and injury. These dogs are racing at over 40mph (65km/h), and a fall at that speed is potentially very serious.

As the race finishes the mechanical hare is quickly covered with a box to stop the dogs pouncing on it and vying to finish it off. The trainers are waiting by the finish post to greet, praise and catch their dogs. The dogs must then be retuned to the secure kennel until the next race is run in case there is a steward's enquiry or a drug test to be done.

So there are six main elements to the likelihood of success in a greyhound race: the grader, the dog (its fitness and state of mind on the day), the trainer's ability, the state of the track, how well the track is managed, and the other dogs and their trainers' ability.

Flapping Tracks

At unregistered or flapping tracks the length of races is the same, but there is no grading system and any dog can be entered in any race. None of the welfare and veterinary support or control is guaranteed.

When Racing is Over

Dogs will often be retired when it is clear they are not going to make the top

During the race each dog must wear a lightweight racing muzzle so that it cannot damage another dog should there be any conflict. Conflict is rare, however. (Photo provided by Nick Guise-Smith www.mirrorboxstudios.co.uk)

grade, though the better ones will race until they are about six years old. Retired greyhounds therefore become available at any age from under a year to seven years old, but most of them are about three or four. A greyhound's normal lifespan is into its early teens, so it still has many good years ahead of it.

Many trainers follow the Greyhound Charter and contact the rescue charities on behalf of a dog's racing owner to arrange for it to come into the charity to be re-homed. Responsible trainers will arrange for the dog to be neutered first, or will ask the racing owner to donate some money to the charity to help with the dog's costs. Greyhound Rescue West of England (GRWE) is one such charity, and details of their work are given in Appendix 1 on page 000.

Less scrupulous trainers and owners have been known to simply abandon retired or unwanted dogs, or to give them away to anyone, whether they are suitable or not. The more conscientious

LOOKING UP A RETIRED GREYHOUND'S PEDIGREE AND RACING HISTORY

Bo Jangles looks up his own pedigree and racing career on the laptop!

If your retired greyhound was raced on a registered track it will have a grand racing name and tattoos in one or both ears. You can use these to find out all about its racing career by using the Greyhound Racing and Breeding Database www.greyhound-data.com; to access the information follow 'Dog Search' or 'Tattoo'. To read the ear tattoos, stand beside the dog and bend the ear back towards you, otherwise you may read the tattoo back to front and upside down – for example, the letters and numbers HN1 would appear INH if you read it from the front of the dog! Also make sure you enter the right-hand ear tattoo in the right box and the left one in the left box. If the tattoos are indistinct, shine a torch through the back of the ear; this will make them show up with amazing clarity.

First your dog's pedigree will appear, going back five generations – which is when you realize what an aristocrat you have living in your home. There will also be a reference to a blood quota of ancestors that appear in its pedigree more than once, and a breakdown of the racing achievements of other dogs that share the same dam (mother); these dogs will be brothers and sisters or half brothers and half sisters to your dog.

Now go to the top of the page and click on 'Races'; there may be a number there too, such as '55 races', so you can see how many times your dog ran. This will open a page with a breakdown of the dog's racing history. Appendix 2 on page 108 gives an example of a typical dog's race history, and goes through this column by column to explain what the data means.

I really enjoy looking up my dogs' racing background. It gives me some insight into their past. Were they top standard or middle of the road, like me? Did they have any bad falls? Were they sprinters or marathon runners? Did they win in spite of being crowded? Why did they retire when they did? Did they run as well as, or better than their parents? The clues are all there, and it is fun to play the detective.

RIGHT: Heather was abandoned in Ireland with her ears cut off so that the tattoos could not be used to trace her back to the people who had abandoned her.

BELOW: After leaving racing Queenie was happy to relax and become a contented member of the family, like most retired greyhounds.

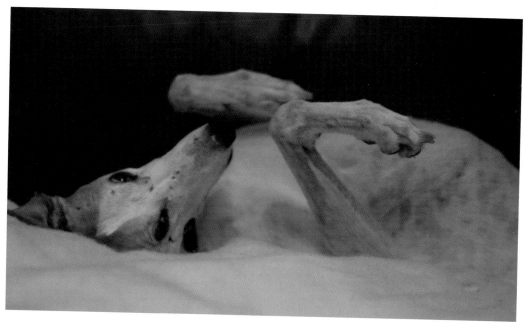

will have these dogs put to sleep following the Greyhound Charter's advice; those less responsible will have them put down by any unlicensed person using often unacceptable methods. It has even been known for some owners or trainers to cut off the tattooed part of a dog's ears before abandoning it so the dog cannot be traced back to them. This sort of practice is becoming less common, but such methods of disposal bring the sport into serious disrepute.

It is estimated that in the region of 10,000 greyhounds retire from racing in any one year. Charities find homes for around 2,000; what is the fate of the rest? It is known that some go for vivisection, and some are exported to Spain where they are run until they are much older; these unfortunate dogs are often kept in very poor conditions with little regard for welfare.

RE-HOMING THE RETIRED GREYHOUND

When you take an ex-racing greyhound into your home you can expect it to know very little about living in a house, or about the world beyond kennels and the race track. It is surprising how well these dogs adjust to their new life; nevertheless it is important to understand how strange it is for them, and to give them time to settle.

AN AGE-OLD ASSOCIATION

Greyhounds have been linked with humans for thousands of years. We have been responsible for their breed development, their good times when they were highly regarded, and their bad times, when they have simply been used as money-making machines. Throughout this time they have remained a dedicated, loyal, affectionate and well-mannered breed. They are wonderful dogs, and their ability to perform as athlete is matched by their ability to subsequently become one of the world's best family pets.

'Safe Flight' (also known as Foxy) enjoying her retirement.

3 IS A GREYHOUND FOR ME?

Before you rush off to take in a retired greyhound, do take a few moments to consider whether it really will be the right dog for you and your family. Having said that, however, there are far more 'pros' than 'cons' to owning a retired greyhound; I have had experience of many different breeds of dog, and they are probably the easiest I have ever owned. I find that males and females are equally easy to care for – even though in this book I refer to individual greyhounds as 'he', it is not because I have any preference but because it is shorter to write! Please bear with me, and if bitches are your favourite, you can always mentally substitute 'she' for 'he'!

THE 'PROS' AND 'CONS' OF OWNERSHIP

Age

Pro: Taking in an adult dog means you will not have to guide it through the very demanding stages of puppyhood.

Con: Your greyhound will have no experience of living in a house, although generally these dogs adapt very quickly. He will need to understand the boundaries in terms of respecting the furnishings and your belongings. However, the same would be true of a puppy, though a puppy takes longer to learn these things, particularly when he is teething and keen to chew anything to hand.

Lead Walking

Pro: Greyhounds are already trained to walk calmly on the lead without pulling.

Con: Having only lived with other greyhounds they may take time to get used to walking quietly past other types of dog, and some may even think small dogs are a potential meal!

Exercise

Pro: Greyhounds do not need much exercise compared with many other breeds. They are sprint dogs, so a short walk and a quick burst of play in the garden is enough for them in the morning, and again in the evening.

Con: It may be some time before your greyhound forgets his racing career enough for you to be able to let him off the lead safely, especially if there are wild rabbits, or the neighbour's cats around. However, he will be quite used to staying on the lead.

Health

Pro: Because greyhounds are built to fulfil a purpose – namely racing, rather than to satisfy breed standards for showing – the breed is free of inbred conditions such as hip dysplasia or breathing problems.

Con: Greyhound races are always raced anti-clockwise and the tracks have sharp

Greyhounds are usually very good with children.

bends so that the dog's 'outside' legs suffer stress during a race; this can lead to arthritis later on in life.

Temperament
Pro: Greyhounds are known for being calm, laid back, affectionate dogs, usually good with children, and they rarely bark.

Con...or is it a pro? A greyhound is unlikely to make it as a guard dog and may not even bark when the doorbell rings.

Recall
Con: Frequently a dog will come from a racing kennels with no idea what its name is, or that it should come to you when you call it (the recall).

Pro: You can change your new dog's name easily, and teaching the recall helps build up a bond between you.

Cleanliness
Pro: Greyhounds have short, fine coats and do not fill your house with hair when they moult.

They have a short, fine coat and will not fill your house with hair.

Pro: Greyhounds are fastidious about keeping themselves clean; they will do anything to avoid a muddy puddle.

Toilet Training

Pro: Greyhounds have usually lived in a kennel with an indoor and an outdoor part, so they will have learned to use the outdoor part for toilet visits. With a little help they will soon learn to go out in your garden for a toilet visit.

Holidays

Pro: Your greyhound will be used to living in kennels, and is unlikely to find going to kennels while you are away at all stressful.

Pro: Greyhounds are used to travelling to race tracks and usually enjoy car travel, so if you wish to take them on holiday with you they will travel well.

ABOVE: Greyhounds are used to travelling to races so most of them really enjoy car travel.

RIGHT: Your retired greyhound will be an aristocratic athlete with a long pedigree.

Greyhounds love to have a soft, thick bed in a cosy corner where they can relax.

Cost

Pro: For the cost of a donation (which all rescues request to help with the cost of neutering and vaccinating the dog) you end up with a well bred pedigree, aristocratic athlete, neutered and vaccinated already, whose breeding details and pedigree you may be able to access on the greyhound racing and breeding website mentioned in the previous chapter.

To Sum Up

Pros: Retired greyhounds are adult, healthy, affectionate, calm, quiet, gentle, easy to keep clean, and they don't need endless exercise.

Cons: They are fast and capable of catching small animals, and have a lot to learn about life outside the kennel.

CONSIDER YOUR LIFESTYLE

If you are thinking of offering a home to a retired greyhound you need to consider whether he will fit in with your lifestyle, and whether you will be a suitable owner for him.

Your House

Is your home suitable? Greyhounds are big dogs, but they do not take up as much space as you would expect. Unlike more lively dogs, such as border collies and terriers which can be forever under your feet, a greyhound is happy to find a quiet space and lie down for most of the day. Have you a space he can call his own, where his bed can be, so that he can go and lie down in peace and quiet if he wants? Do you have laminate flooring? Most greyhounds find this too slippery to walk on and you may need to put down a mat.

What is a Suitable Age?

Greyhounds suit all ages of people. Because they are so gentle and don't require endless exercise they are often better suited to older people than the more energetic breeds such as terriers and collies. An older person is also less likely to trip over a greyhound than they are a smaller dog. If you want a greyhound but cannot walk it, you can find help through the Cinnamon Trust; they have registered volunteers who will give elderly or ill people support so they can keep their pets. Greyhounds do get on well with people of all ages, though they sometimes find crawling babies and toddlers rather scary and outside their range of understanding. To a dog, a toddler crawling towards him can look predatory. However, it is important to be aware that no dog of any breed should ever be left alone with a young child.

Do You Need a Garden?

Do you have a garden? Some rescues will consider homing dogs to a home with no garden, but it is not ideal. For example, if you don't have an easily accessible garden, consider the thought of having to get dressed again after you have had a nice warm bath and are ready to snuggle up in bed with a good book, to take the dog round the block before it settles for the night. Can you cope with this?

Fencing

How well is your garden fenced? Greyhounds will not jump great heights or crawl on their bellies to escape, but they will squeeze through holes, and if a greyhound sees a cat on the other side of the fence it will throw caution to the wind in its efforts to get through. As with any dog, it is important that he cannot escape from the garden, which ideally should have a good solid fence that is at least 5ft (2m) high. Obviously the gate must also be high enough for him not to be able to jump it!

If your garden is easily overlooked from the road it will not be safe to leave your dog out in the garden alone. Many are stolen from people's gardens every year, especially pedigree dogs or fast dogs that could be used for coursing.

Garden Space

How much space is there for the dog? A small paved garden cluttered up with pots and garden furniture is not very dog-friendly. Greyhounds often like to have a 'funny five minutes' when they hurtle madly round in all directions, spinning and skidding, full of the sheer joy of living. It is a wonderful performance to

Molly demonstrates that a 'funny five minutes' requires plenty of space.

watch, but to do this safely they need space. A small garden is fine as long as it is not crammed with objects the dog can damage himself on.

Your Working Hours

How long are your working hours? Many adult greyhounds have spent long hours in kennels with the company of other dogs but without continuous contact with people. There is a good chance then that they will be able to cope with you going off to work for two or three hours, though an eight-hour day is too long. If you have to work longer than four hours at a stretch, maybe you could organize a professional dog walker to come and take him out. Or perhaps a reliable neighbour is looking for a dog to walk. There are tips later on in this book for times when you have to leave your dog at home. If you are going to offer a home to a greyhound, make sure that you read

Children and greyhounds can make lovely playmates.

Chapter 9 'Problem Solving' so that you can manage leaving your dog successfully right from the start.

Exercise

Are you a family that likes to walk miles? A greyhound will love to be part of such a family – though be aware that you will need to build up the distances slowly. Remember he has been a sprint dog, and may find a route march on his first day too much – he may even get sore paw pads. Greyhounds are quite lazy dogs, and after a short walk and a sprint round the garden they are generally happy to sleep for a few hours.

Your Patience

Always bear in mind that it is very unlikely that a retired greyhound is going to fit into your home perfectly right from day one. Adjustments will need to be made by both humans and greyhound during the first few weeks until harmony is achieved. There will be some training involved, and there will be moments when you ask yourself if you have done the right thing. Have you enough patience to see the settling-in period through?

CHILDREN AND GREYHOUNDS

Generally greyhounds are very good with children: they are gentle and calm, but they also love to play wild games with them out in the garden. Children and greyhounds often make inseparable companions, and this sort of friendship is a wonderful experience for a child. However, be aware that a toddler can easily be knocked over when a big dog such as a greyhound is having a boisterous moment – though usually there is no harm done and the toddler learns to walk in spite of his enthusiastic friend. Also when your greyhound first comes out of racing he will potentially be too strong for a child to walk on the lead, should he see, for example, a rabbit or a cat. You will need to assess this situation before letting a child walk him.

GREYHOUNDS AND OTHER DOGS

If you have ever attended a meeting of rescue greyhounds (and it is a really good idea to do so if you are considering taking one into your home) you will notice that although there may be around sixty greyhounds all in one small village hall, there is rarely an argument among them. The only time you might hear a dog being aggressive, you will usually find it is a visiting dog of another breed.

At the end of this book is a list of greyhound rescue/retirement web sites. You can look up their events pages if you would like to attend an event and mingle with a few greyhounds and greyhound owners.

Having lived in racing kennels all its life a greyhound may find another breed of dog very strange. Some have docked tails, others are covered in hair, yet more have long droopy ears, and a greyhound will find it hard to read their body

A group of owners and greyhounds enjoying a flag day. When greyhounds are together they almost never argue.

ABOVE: Most greyhounds are happy to be part of a group of various breeds. (Photo by Nicola Feltham www.nfelthamp hotography.co.uk)

LEFT: Greyhounds love the companionship of another dog, and will soon settle in with a new pal.

language at first and will wonder whether it is friend or foe...or *dinner*! There are tips to help you with this later in the book.

If you already have another dog – of whatever breed – when you first go to look at your potential new greyhound, you should take your other dog with you so that they can meet on neutral ground.

Greyhounds love the companionship of another dog and usually settle in well with a new pal.

GREYHOUNDS AND OTHER ANIMALS

Many people think greyhounds cannot live with small pets or livestock, however mine live with me on a smallholding with ducks, sheep, horses and chickens. Some are safe enough to come in the chicken pen or the sheep paddock with me, while others have to be left outside. It does not cause a problem, and it is easy just to shut the gate. But if you decide to be a greyhound owner you must take responsibility for keeping your dog from chasing other people's livestock.

Many greyhounds live in homes with securely caged guinea pigs and rabbits (it helps if the cages are raised off the ground). I know of two greyhounds that live with house rabbits, and quite a few that live with cats. Some rescue groups will 'cat-test' greyhounds before they home them, to see if there is a possibility that they may be tolerant towards cats. They will then advise you how best to introduce your cat-tested greyhound to your cat.

Remember that for all the years the greyhound has raced, chasing small furry things has been the right thing to do; it is what he has been bred for. It is very unfair to expect a greyhound to suddenly change his instinctive responses, so please don't be cross with him when he chases. Later in the book you will find advice on walking him past small furry things.

Responsible greyhound charities will re-home the dog to you with a basket muzzle, which he should wear whenever he goes out of the house during the first few weeks until you know what his response to small furry things will be.

If you are really squeamish about the fact that he may, one day, bring you a mangled dead rabbit, then a greyhound is not for you.

LOOKING FOR THE RIGHT ONE

There is no doubt that going through a recognized greyhound rescue charity will give you a better chance of getting the right dog than homing one straight from the track. All the dogs from rescue charities should have been vaccinated, microchipped and neutered. They will have been assessed in various situations, and experienced people will help match you up with the right dog.

Some greyhounds live comfortably alongside all sorts of other livestock, including chickens.

With a coat like velvet: a healthy, well groomed black greyhound absolutely shines.

If you have cats and small pets, then it is best to look for one that has never raced or is still very young – less than a year old – and not too keen. However, sometimes older dogs that have been tested as tolerant towards cats will be available.

If you go out to work then it may be best to look at an older dog that is not going to be bursting with energy and looking for mischief while you are out.

Some people prefer male dogs and some females, and opinions abound as to the faithfulness or calmness of each sex. I have had plenty of both and I have honestly found no difference. Furthermore, if they have been castrated or speyed, their sexual behaviour is not apparent. What sex the dog is would be the last question on my list; I would be much more concerned about its temperament and appearance.

The same goes for colour. Around 50

per cent of greyhounds are black, as this is the dominant colour – yet many people (28 per cent in a survey I carried out in 2008) do not like black dogs. There is no sensible reasoning behind this preference, as black dogs have just as good a temperament as any other colour. One thing is certain, and that is that black dogs always end up with the sleekest, shiniest-looking coats!

If you already have a dog it is sometimes easier if you get the new dog of the opposite sex as they are more likely to get on, but this isn't guaranteed – and what happens if you have three dogs…? Many homes have a group of male dogs, or a group of bitches or a mixed group with no trouble.

Just like us, greyhounds have different personalities. Some are confident and greet you happily, and in spite of having always lived in kennels they cope with the outside world very well. Some are timid and need a little more time to adjust and be brave enough to greet you. Some appear aloof because they are unsure of what is going on, and prefer to hang back and see what happens. Each personality will soon learn to live happily in a home, but you may have a preference as to which sort of dog you would like to offer a home to.

PREPARATION

If you have got as far as this section you have probably decided to go ahead with offering a home to a retired greyhound. I think you will be very pleased with your decision. Not only will you have a lovely, calm, handsome, pedigree dog living in your home, but you will have given a home to a dog whose fate might have been, sadly, very different if it wasn't for you!

Your greyhound will need the following equipment:

- A collar
- ID tags
- A lead
- A soft bed
- A raised food bowl
- A water bowl
- Training treats
- Toys
- A coat

A collar: You can get smart, wide leather collars for outdoors and soft martingale collars for indoors if you wish. Never use a check chain on any dog, but especially not on a greyhound: they have such a thin pelt that a check chain can tear their neck in seconds. Both collars need identity tags on them. A large greyhound will need a size 6 at least, and a small one will need a size 5. If the dog you are going to re-home is particularly nervous, it is a good idea to get a harness for walking it: when in a panic, nervous dogs can sometimes slip their collar.

ID tags for each collar: You can get these made up at ironmongers, pet shops and key cutters. An ID tag is a legal requirement and must have your surname, address and phone number on it. This is essential in the early days when the dog is most likely to stray. Generally it is not a good idea to put their own name on the tag, in case they are stolen. It is essential to include your mobile number in case you lose the dog while you are away on holiday, or so that whoever finds the dog can contact you when you are out looking for it. Better still, don't lose the dog!

A lead: This should be of strong leather or webbing. Never use an extending lead with a ratchet. A greyhound can do 0 to 46mph (0 to 74 kph) in 6sec, and by the time they reach the end of the extending lead (and before you can apply the ratchet) they are at full speed. The result can be a broken arm for you or a broken neck for the dog.

A nice soft bed: An old duvet and cover is ideal, or you can buy a big soft dog bed fairly cheaply from a pet stall at the local market. Greyhounds tend to be more comfortable on a big open bed on which they can spread themselves out, than on a circular, preformed bed. You also need to give some thought

as to where your dog will sleep. It is best if he can have a cosy niche to call his own, rather than a place where people are stepping over or round him all the time.

A raised food bowl on a stand: Greyhounds are deep chested and it is uncomfortable for them to eat off ground level. You can buy these bowls and stands in most pet shops.

A water bowl: You can buy stands that hold two bowls, one for water and one for food. Dogs need to have access to water at all times.

The basic equipment your greyhound will need.

A properly fitted coat will keep your greyhound warm and dry in the winter.

Some suitable food: A 'complete' diet with 20 per cent protein or less is best for greyhounds. Too much protein can make them hyperactive. Greyhounds can also have a sensitive stomach, so are often better suited to foods lower in colours and flavourings.

Some treats and toys: Use treats for training, and toys to enrich his new life with you. Greyhounds love soft toys, but be aware that they often love them to pieces!

A coat: In the winter, because greyhounds have such thin fur and very little body fat, they do feel the cold. Your greyhound may need a fleece to wear at night if your heating goes off, and another for braving the colder weather outside. It is best to buy the coat after you have got the dog, as you will need to measure it to make sure it is the right size. Coats that are made for other breeds of dog are far too big round the middle for greyhounds. Retired greyhound charities have merchandise catalogues and web sites where you can buy tailor-made greyhound coats for indoors and outdoors.

IN CONCLUSION

If you have decided to offer a retired greyhound a home you will need to contact one of the retired/rescued greyhound charities. Their details can be found at the back of this book. You might even consider having two greyhounds. I think two are even easier than one, as then they have company of their own kind!

I am convinced that owning two greyhounds is easier than one.

4 THE ADOPTION PROCESS

SOURCES

It is possible to adopt greyhounds direct from some trainers, but remember that a rescue charity wants to find the right home for the right dog, whereas a man who offers you a dog at the race track simply wants to home the dog. Unscrupulous trainers have been known to put pressure on unwary adopters by saying that if they do not take the dog it will be put to sleep. This is very difficult to resist, but good owners and trainers will make proper provision for their dog by arranging for it to go to one of the rescue charities. Such dogs have usually been better handled and better cared for than those that are handed over irresponsibly, and are the sort of dogs that will make better pets.

All responsible charities for the re-homing of ex-racing greyhounds (sometimes referred to as 'rescue' and sometimes as 'retired') will vaccinate, neuter and microchip the greyhound before they look for a home for it. They will also have it vet-checked and make sure it has been treated for worms or fleas. It will then be kennelled or fostered while it is assessed to see which home would suit it best, and what problems it might have, if any. This costs the charity around £350 to £500 for each dog, depending on the length of its stay in kennels and whether any extra vet's costs are incurred. When you home a dog from a charity they will ask you to pay a donation. Most people pay around £100. This is excellent value for money. If you take a dog direct from a trainer it is a leap in the dark as far as the dog's personality and health is concerned, and you will have to spend around £300 to get it vaccinated and neutered. Unless the trainer is someone you know, or is recommended to you by someone you trust, it is much safer and cheaper to go down the rescue/retired greyhound charity route. If possible choose a charity that is a member of the Association of Cats and Dogs Homes (ACDH).

So where do charities find the rest of the money to pay for 'processing' a dog? The charities are run purely by a community of volunteers. Some of the volunteers are responsible for fund raising to cover the rest of the dog's expenses. They run flag days, quiz nights, fêtes, fairs, dog shows, dog walks and all sorts of other innovative events to raise money and raise the profile of retired greyhounds as pets. Belonging to these charities is great fun and you can join in as little or as much as you want. I do voluntary work for the largest independent greyhound rescue charity in England, and I love attending our stall at shows with my greyhounds and meeting dog lovers from all walks of life. It is possible that opening your home to a greyhound will open up a whole new life for you among like-minded people – but you can home a

Dogs and owners alike seem to enjoy fundraising for their greyhound charity.

Three matching greyhounds in Santa costumes collecting for their re-homing charity at Christmas.

Attending charity events with your dog often helps you bond with him, and meet new friends as well.

greyhound and have no further connection with the charity if you prefer.

Responsible charities will give you support through your first days of owning a dog. The charity I work with makes contact with you a day or two after you have homed the dog, to see how things are going, and again four months later. They may also provide people qualified in behaviour work with whom you can consult, free of charge, should you have a problem.

My advice therefore would be to go to one of the charities listed in the back of this book to find your retired greyhound.

'PROCESSING' A DOG

Most charities have similar procedures to the one I work with. Once a dog has been handed over to us – from whatever source – it will have a busy week or two going to the vets to be neutered, vaccinated and microchipped. Its teeth and nails will be checked and dealt with if necessary, and it will be wormed, checked and, where necessary, treated for fleas.

Once this has been done it may be sent on to one of our charities' 'outposts' – kennels in another area where it stands a good chance of finding a home.

While waiting for its final vaccination and to have the stitches removed from the neutering operation, the dog will be walked by volunteers who will assess its behaviour on the lead, its keenness with livestock and birds, and its reaction to other dogs and to people coming into the kennel. Where possible we will see how well it gets on with children. It will also be tested for its reaction to cats. Cat-friendly dogs are not plentiful, and are usually reserved for people who own cats. It is not likely that you will be given a cat-friendly dog just because a relative

or neighbour has a cat. In any case, most cat-friendly greyhounds will respect only the cat they live with, and regard the rest as fair game.

The assessments help the re-homing officer to make informed decisions about which dog to recommend to which home. We still don't know everything about the dog, but we do our best to tell prospective owners everything we do know. We don't want a dog to go to a home which is not right for it, any more than a prospective owner wants a dog that is not right for them.

THE HOME CHECK

Good rescue centres will not home a dog with you unless they have done a home check. There is nothing to fear regarding this process. A representative of the charity will visit you, and will usually take a greyhound along too, for you to meet. They will want to know where the dog is going to have his bed, whether the garden is securely fenced, and how many hours the dog will be left on its own on a regular basis. Many greyhounds are successfully homed to people who work, especially if someone can come and let the dog out or take it for a walk if it is going to be left for more than three or four hours. An older dog will cope with this situation better than a young one will.

The home check is also an opportunity for you to ask questions and discuss exactly what you are looking for in your new dog.

The home checker may not tell you if you have passed your home check immediately, as she/he may need to discuss details with the re-homing officer before a joint decision is made. Most people pass the home check with flying colours, so please don't be concerned about this process, but use it as a time to ask questions and to find out all you want to know.

By the time you have passed your home check a lot of volunteers have put time and effort into processing your application. They will be disappointed if you then get a dog from elsewhere. If you are going to apply for a dog it is more helpful to stay committed to one charity while they find you the ideal dog, than to keep swapping around.

HOW MUCH CHOICE?

Years ago you would turn up at a charity kennels and walk through looking at the dogs. You would then pick a dog that looked nice to you, however unsuitable it might be for your lifestyle. Nine times out of ten, a few weeks later you would hand the dog back in, utterly disappointed and demoralized because it hadn't worked out for you.

Most charities are more careful now. After your home check the re-homing officer will look at the dogs in kennels and mentally weed out all the unsuitable ones. You will then be invited to kennels by appointment to meet the dog or dogs most suited to you and your home environment. If you like a dog it can become yours. But if you are not sure, you will not be pressurized to take it. The re-homing officer wants happy owners and a happy dog. It is very unsettling for the dog to be returned, so everyone tries to get a perfect match. Re-homing officers are usually very experienced and have worked in various capacities within the charity for many years before they get to be re-homing officers, so do trust their judgement.

At first you may be disappointed that you are not going to be offered a wide choice, but it stops you falling in love with totally the wrong dog.

Most charities do have dogs for re-homing featured on their web sites. This helps you to express a preference for a dog, but bear in mind that if you have seen a dog you like on the web site, so have hundreds of other people all round the country, and that dog may be re-homed fairly quickly to someone else. However, dogs on the web site are often just a taster, and in the kennels are other very similar dogs just waiting to be the one chosen to curl up by your fireside!

When you go to see a dog you should take everyone in your immediate family, and any dogs you already own, to meet it. It is a good idea to take it for a short walk and give it time to get to know your present dog on neutral territory.

FOLLOW-UP SUPPORT

A good rescue charity will keep in touch with you after you have taken the dog home so you don't feel that you are coping on your own should anything go wrong. The rescue charity I work with makes sure you receive a phone call a day or two after you have taken the dog home to check how things are going and to give advice if you need it.

We also do a four-month post-homing check. Your home checker will make an appointment to come and see you and your dog after four months to help with any problems and answer any questions. We also have a help line with free access to people qualified in behaviour work who can help you through any problems that arise.

It is best to choose a charity that offers you this sort of support, and don't be afraid to use it. It is much better to ask for help early on, than allow a small, solvable problem to spiral into something much bigger.

OWNERSHIP RULES OF VARIOUS CHARITIES

Most charities will tell you that the dog is yours for life now: you make all the decisions about its lifestyle and medication. When the dog grows old, the day may come when you have to make that awful final decision – but it is your decision to make. However, a good charity will also insist that if, for any reason, you reach a time when you can no longer keep the dog, it cannot be passed on but must be returned to the charity.

From the moment the dog has entered our charity kennels we have taken responsibility for it. We delegate that responsibility to you, but we are there in the background as back-up should you be unable to continue taking responsibility. That is our promise to the dog.

IF THINGS GO WRONG

So can you return the dog if things go wrong? Ideally you are offering your greyhound a home for life. Changes of home cause dogs a great deal of distress, and you need to be completely committed to helping your greyhound settle in your home and to looking after him for the rest of his life. If the regional homing officer feels you are not committed enough or have any doubts, she or he will ask you to go away and think further about your decision before you take a dog.

It is very wrong to take a dog home for a 'trial period' and then change your mind as soon as it does something you don't like. Each time a dog is returned, mental 'baggage' is added to its pile, and its likelihood of finding a home becomes

One of our charity's dogs waiting patiently at kennels for Mr and Mrs 'Right' to offer him a home.

more compromised. Some dogs are returned because their owner dies or becomes seriously ill, and some because of marriage splits or other life-changing problems. These cannot be avoided, and the sensible option is to return the dog. However, the dog is going to become a member of your family, and you should ask yourself, would you give your children back if they wet the bed, or had a fight with another child? No, of course you wouldn't, and your dog should have the same consideration.

TO SUM UP

- It is wiser to get a retired greyhound from a rescue/retirement charity.
- A responsible charity will vaccinate, microchip and neuter the dog prior to homing.
- A responsible charity will give post-homing support, and will also insist the dog is returned to the charity should you not be able to keep him.
- Your retired greyhound is yours for life, with all the responsibilities that go with it.

5 THE FIRST FEW DAYS

A STEEP LEARNING CURVE

Your new greyhound has probably never lived in a house before, so everything will be new and strange. He is finding out about televisions, vacuum cleaners, glass doors and mirrors for the first time, so naturally it will take him some time to settle in. Greyhounds new to homes see no reason why they shouldn't stand on the dining-room table to get a better look out of the window! They are not being naughty, they are just exploring their new environment. They are undergoing a huge culture shock, and it may well be one for you, too! The best way to help is to be calm and to give him/her time to explore without making any demands. Please never get cross with your greyhound if he does something you don't like. This book will help you to understand and deal with these situations. Remember he is not being naughty, he is just coping with this huge change in the best way he knows how.

When you first arrive home, take your dog on the lead into the garden to the place you want him to use for a toilet, and wait with him (for however long it

Roger on his first time in a house coming to terms with television.

Finding a chew or a pig's ear waiting for him on his new bed will help your new greyhound to decide his bed is a nice place to be.

takes) until he performs. Praise him immediately – a titbit is often well received – and then take him to explore the garden boundaries before going indoors.

With the help of your home checker you should have designated a safe, quiet, warm place to put down a soft, thick bed for your dog. Unless you have another dog you could have a chew or a pig's ear waiting for him on the bed so that he naturally goes there for comfort. However, if you have a dog already, this is not a good idea because most spats between dogs happen over food.

Respect his space when he is in his bed, and make it a 'no go' area for children. He needs somewhere to call his own where he can chill out when it all gets too much for him. Resist the urge to keep calling him, and especially ask children to leave him in peace on his first day. Children will often call and call a dog for no reason, and without giving him any reward, so that he quickly becomes deadened to his own name and stops responding to any recall.

TOILET TRAINING

Keep a close watch on your dog so that you can start toilet training straightaway. Dogs will not usually foul in their bed area unless they are very stressed. In kennels they will naturally use the outdoor run, but in your house they have no idea where to go. So every three hours, or if you see your dog mooching around restlessly, or if you have just fed your dog, or if he has just woken up, put him on the lead, take him in the garden to the designated toilet place and stay with him (however long it takes) until he has performed.

Praise/reward him and take him for a little game or a walk round as a reward too, before you go back in. (Otherwise if he always goes straight back in after he has performed he may delay the performance to get more time in the garden!) The more consistent you are with this, the quicker a dog will learn. It is all down to you. It can be done in forty-eight hours if you work hard enough at it, though some dogs take longer to learn than others.

Never scold or punish your dog for going to the toilet in the house. He is not being naughty: he simply doesn't understand what you want yet. He will respond by learning to do it when you are not looking because he knows it makes you angry but he can't see why it should. He may even find places to hide it – such as behind the sofa to avoid your anger! He may also decide that as it is not safe to do it while you are around, he will stop doing it when you are outside with him.

A dog that soils constantly in the house or in its bed area is possibly very stressed. The less stressed you can be about this issue, the sooner the dog will settle.

SETTLING IN

The First Meal
Your new greyhound may feel too stressed to tuck into his first few meals. Don't worry; he won't starve himself to death! Don't try to coax him to eat, either. If he feels too nervous to eat and you are holding his food bowl and crooning to him, you will only make him feel worse. Put the bowl of food down and walk away. After twenty minutes take the bowl of food away and offer the dog nothing till the next mealtime. Leaving the bowl down will only teach him that he can pick and choose when to eat, and if he is stressed he doesn't want to have to make decisions. Don't worry about trying to make the meal more palatable: it isn't the taste that is worrying the dog, it is the change of circumstances, and only time can heal that.

The First Night
Giving the dog his own bed downstairs at night will help him to learn that there are times when you can't be with him and he must settle on his own. Do expect that you may have an interrupted night. It is also a good idea to explain to your neighbours and to ask them to bear with you for the first couple of nights.

Before you go to bed take your dog out for his last toilet visit. Take him on the lead. At some kennels the greyhounds are kept warm at night using heat lamps which give off a warm light, so they are often not used to going out in complete darkness and will easily panic. For this reason it may help if at first you leave a small night light on in the room where he sleeps.

Although your dog may have a soft warm bed, be aware that greyhounds have thin coats and their backs soon get cold. If it is winter and your heating goes off at night he will be cold. Covering him with a blanket will not work as dogs turn round in the night just as we do, but they don't have hands to catch hold of the blanket and take it with them as we do. On cold nights your dog will therefore need a warm fleece greyhound jacket: you can find out more about these from the merchandise web sites listed in the back of this book.

Don't make a fuss when you leave him for the night. You could leave him with something safe to chew if he is not shar-

In the winter your greyhound will appreciate a nice warm fleece to keep him cosy on cold nights.

ing with another dog. It is usually safer to keep dogs that are new to each other in separate rooms for the first few nights, or use an indoor kennel for one of them, until they are settled and living in harmony.

If your dog cries, try to ignore it. If you go down to him whenever he cries or scratches the door, he will know that he has found the best way to make you come to him, and he will never settle. If you have a dog that really won't settle after an hour or two, you may feel the need to come down and sleep near him, but don't acknowledge him. Give him the comfort of having someone nearby without giving him the reward of your attention. Just be there, but say nothing and don't look at him. If you take him upstairs with you it will make it even harder to go back to leaving him downstairs.

How well you manage on the first night sets the pattern for the future. After all, he slept in kennels on his own so he is used to being alone at night – though he did have the security of other dogs nearby. Please don't get cross with

him: he is crying because he is distressed and bewildered, and you will only make him feel worse.

If your dog continues to find it difficult to go through the night without disturbing you, you will find some more tips in Chapter 9 Problem Solving.

HELPING CHILDREN TO GET IT RIGHT

It is important with any breed of dog that children respect a dog's need for his own space: just like us, he sometimes has an 'off' day when he needs some peace and quiet. As well as making his bed a 'no go' area for children, be aware too that if he has a favourite place such as a hearth rug or sofa, he just may take exception to a child invading this space. A dog that feels his space invaded will freeze for a moment; his eyes will become 'hard', and he may growl or slope off somewhere. Children need to know that they must move away when this happens. If the dog has been through his warning repertoire and the child has not moved away, he has no other course left to him than to snap. And is he really to blame?

We also need to remember that any rescue dog, of whatever breed, may have lived on the edge of starvation. Greyhounds are kept down to a minimum weight when in racing, and those that are subsequently abandoned have to scavenge for survival. A child walking around with food may therefore be vulnerable as the dog may snatch the food and frighten or hurt the child in the process. While he is settling in it is better to ask children to sit up to the table when they are eating, where they will be safe. They also need to know the rule never to go near any dog when it is eating, whether it's food, or a titbit, or bone.

Greyhounds can reach 0 to 46mph (74km/h) in six seconds. For this reason it is best if an adult walks the dog on the lead at first so that an assessment can be made as to whether a child is capable of walking the dog; or put the dog on a second lead so the child can walk the dog with you.

Much of this guidance for children applies with any dog, not just a greyhound, so don't be put off; if children follow the rules it helps to keep them safe. What is most important is that young children should never be left unsupervised with any dog. Be aware that some dogs find crawling babies and toddlers quite frightening, and are not sure how to react.

To summarize:

- Help children to learn when a dog is giving a warning, and to move away.
- Ask children to respect the dog's resting space.
- It is not safe to allow children to walk the dog.
- Do not allow children to wander around eating in front of the dog.
- Children need to know never to go near a dog when it is eating.
- Never leave young children unsupervised with a dog.

Greyhounds are usually incredibly patient and loving towards children. They make wonderful confidantes, and are better than most breeds at being a dependable playmate.

Greyhounds can reach from 0 to 46mph in six seconds.

OUT AND ABOUT

The First Walk

Most greyhound charities will give you a muzzle when they home a greyhound with you. These are usually the plastic basket type, and dogs can comfortably pant, drink and be given titbits in these. In the early days it is best to put the muzzle on whenever you take the dog out for a walk, until you have assessed his response to other animals you may meet on your walks. As soon as you pick up his lead your greyhound may become wildly excited. In kennels this may have been his only chance of seeing anything of the world outside. Some new greyhounds go the other way and become very scared of the adventure. If he is wildly excited, wait calmly, saying nothing, until he settles before you put the lead on. If you reward him by trying to put the lead on when he is leaping about he will get even more excitable next time.

Follow the same waiting routine for putting on the muzzle and for going out of the door so that it is clear he will not get his walk until he is co-operative. It may take a while the first two or three times, but it will make it much easier and will save hours of battle in the future! If you have a very nervous dog, don't try to reassure him, he will think you are confirming his fear. Be matter of fact about getting him ready for the walk, and start with little walks, building up to longer ones as his confidence grows.

The first walk with you will be full of wonder for your greyhound: the place is new, all the animals he meets will seem strange, and he may not be used to traffic. You are also new to him, and he doesn't know if he can trust you to keep him safe, so keep the walk short and of course

A basket-type muzzle should be used in the early days while you assess your greyhound's response to new animals and situations. Basket muzzles are best because they allow the dog to pant and drink.

do not let him off the lead: it is far too early for that.

If your greyhound were a puppy it would be best to let him have a long lead and socialize with other dogs. However, this is a different scenario. Your greyhound may not have seen other breeds of dog, and if you let him go in front of you towards the other dogs he may feel that you are putting him in the front line. The first time you come across another dog, position yourself so that you are between your greyhound and the other dog, shorten the lead and keep walking firmly, taking your greyhound with you. Make no fuss. Your body language is telling him 'We are not bothered about other dogs'. Keep going, even if he wants to bark or go towards the other dog.

When you have passed the other dog – if he has gone past quietly – praise him. If he has made a fuss, ignore this behaviour. Don't ever be tempted to tell your dog off or to get cross with the other dog or its owner: you will simply appear to your dog as if you are joining in, and he will

Find a safe enclosed space to let your greyhound off the lead.

feel that he was right to be stressed because you are, too. Keeping calm is the key to getting your dog's co-operation in everything.

When your dog has been walking with you for some weeks and knows that you are going to take him past other dogs safely, you can relax more. It is often a nuisance when you meet other people whose dogs are off the lead and come running over. Your dog is not ready to go off the lead safely yet, and feels vulnerable because he is on the lead and can't make his own decision whether to escape or not. By keeping walking you are helping him with this decision. Strangely enough, if you stick your head in the air and keep going, other dogs will often give up and go away.

If your greyhound is not used to traffic, try to stay on quieter roads with increasing access to slightly busier roads, and build up to traffic gently. If your dog becomes really stressed you have taken it too fast. Go back a step. Again your calmness will help him. Don't try to comfort or

sympathize with him: be strong for him. By walking calmly and ignoring him, show him there is nothing to be afraid of. And whenever he has walked past calmly, you can praise him.

The Recall

Retired greyhounds often have no idea what their name is, nor has it been necessary for them to learn the recall. However, for your dog's safety, the sooner you start teaching him this, the better.

Try not to use his name unnecessarily, and only combine it with a nice experience: using his name crossly is a waste of time. He has a choice whether he comes to you or not. If someone called you sternly, would you want to go to them? You need to back up your use of his name to get him to come with instant rewards. Practise at home and in the garden. It will take some time before you are ready to let him off the lead. Before you think of doing so, make sure you have read about teaching the recall; this is covered more fully in Chapter 10, Obedience Training.

Remember he has just come out of racing. His boring kennel days were lit up by the chance to run with other dogs and chase a lure. However nice you are to be with, when he spots a rabbit it will be that 'Daddy or chips moment'. You may remember the television advertisement where two sisters are sitting down to tea with a plate each of famous oven chips. The older sister says, 'Which do you like best, Daddy or chips?' We know the little girl loves her Dad, but she is hungry and the chips are right in front of her, hot and tasty, and she can smell them. She finds it really difficult to decide at that moment between them. So, your greyhound sees a rabbit, you call him; he thinks, 'Rabbit or owner. In those early days you are never going to win! So do not let him off the lead for a few months unless you are in a safely enclosed space.

OTHER DOGS IN THE HOUSE

It may be that your greyhound is going to be lucky enough to have another canine companion when he comes to live with you. There is no doubt to me that two dogs are easier than one, and two greyhounds are easiest of all. Dogs settle far better when you go out if they have one of their own for company. Or it may be that you will regularly have other dogs visiting. Most dogs slot into living together with no trouble at all. Following the guidelines below will help it happen smoothly.

A group of greyhounds will easily live happily together.

When two dogs are going to meet, whether it is when your present dog meets your prospective new greyhound, or when your visiting dog arrives, the best procedure is the same: first choose neutral territory for the meeting. After all, if someone marched uninvited into your home you would feel defensive, and a resident dog will feel the same.

Have both dogs on the lead, and a muzzle on the new greyhound. Ask someone to walk one of the dogs while you walk the other. Have both dogs on the outside so that the people are walking next to each other. Don't allow the dogs to walk in front of you towards each other: that way you are putting them both in the front line.

Go straight into walking purposefully beside each other so that both dogs are walking parallel to each other, and each is being encouraged to concentrate on the walk, and not the other dog. If all goes well, swap one dog to the inside. If all continues to go well, put the other dog to the inside and keep walking. By the time you have walked for about five or ten minutes both dogs will have had a chance to look at each other without feeling threatened, so now you can relax and let them have more interaction.

If you have followed this procedure when taking your present dog to meet your prospective greyhound at kennels, the next step is to put them in the car to travel home together. Leave the muzzle on the greyhound so that you can have peace of mind whilst driving. Don't force two strange dogs to share a tiny space at this stage, but travel them separately if need be.

When you get home, or in the case of a visiting dog, once you have been for your introductory walk, take both dogs in the garden and let them mooch around off the lead. There may be some chasing at this stage, so make sure you have removed any garden furniture that the dogs might hurt themselves on in the fun of the chase. When they have settled down, take them indoors. Keep the greyhound's muzzle on till you are sure they are settled with each other.

Never expect two strange dogs to share toys, food bowls or confined spaces safely in the early days, and be careful with treats. When you feed two dogs always stand between them until they have finished their food, and don't allow the first one that finishes to walk over to the dog that is still eating. With two strange dogs of any breed these situations need careful handling. After the dogs have lived together comfortably for a week or two you will be able to relax your guard.

Two dogs learning to live together will have arguments, but these will rarely be serious. Allow them to sort out their differences as far as possible. The less you interfere, the sooner they will be able to sort things out between them. Human interference will often make things worse. Sometimes one dog might cause the other an injury, but often that signals the end of the conflict, so don't be hasty and think it is not working. Give them time to learn to live together.

Many people make the mistake of thinking they should be extra nice to their first dog so that he doesn't feel he is being pushed out. On the contrary, treat the dogs equally. If you make a bigger fuss of the first dog or favour it, you will cause further conflict.

LEARNING THE HOUSE RULES

Day one is a good time to decide what the house rules are. It may be that you have decided that you don't want the

A greyhound will make a beeline for your sofa, so decide before that happens whether the sofa is to be a 'no go' area or not.

A stair gate is really helpful in keeping your dogs from going upstairs or in rooms you don't want them to use.

dog to go upstairs or to go on the sofa, so start the way you mean to go on. The best way to make the rule is to make these places unavailable. If your dog tries to get on the sofa gently push him away without making eye contact or talking to him. If you are going to be out of the room leave a few books strewn on the sofa so that it would be uncomfortable to lie on. Greyhounds are notorious as sofa lovers so he will try really hard to get you to give in! Some people have a sofa for the greyhound and a sofa for themselves!

Greyhounds are not very proficient at going up and especially down stairs because they are so gangly, but they soon learn. If you would like him to stay downstairs a stair gate is a good idea, or if your stairs are in the hallway, shutting the door that gives access to the stairs is easy. If the dog does wander upstairs and you would prefer him not to, don't reward him by greeting him and speaking to him: simply take him back down again straightaway. You may have to do it a few times, but he should soon catch on.

All dogs of any breed find changes difficult, and coming to live in a house with unknown people may be stressful for your dog. It may also be stressful for you. It is a miracle that most dogs slot in as if they have always been there. If the first few days are stressful, please be patient, and consistent with what you ask of him. You will soon understand your dog better and he will learn what you need, too, and then things will settle down.

CAT-FRIENDLY GREYHOUNDS

If you have a cat at home and have asked for a cat-friendly greyhound you still have to plan very carefully how you introduce it to your cat. The cat-test that the dog has been through at kennels is no guarantee that it will live well with your cat. It is simply an indication that, given the right circumstances, it may settle down with a cat.

In the charity I work for the greyhound cat-test is done in one room. The doors are shut so that the cat cannot escape. One volunteer holds the dog on a lead and muzzled. The other holds the cat. The dog is watched to see its reaction. If the dog is obviously keen to go for the cat at any stage in the proceedings the test is stopped. Some dogs show no interest in the cat initially and are far more interested in exploring the house.

The cat is then put down and encouraged to run and jump. Dogs that are not cat-friendly will get wildly excited at this, and the test ends. If the dog still shows no reaction, or if he demonstrates a politely wagging-tail interest, the test progresses. The cat is picked up again and the dog is allowed to move forwards to meet it, still wearing muzzle and lead. This is where some cats will give the dog a smack on the nose, whilst others will want to disappear. Some dogs, having been given a smack on the nose, decide to have nothing to do with cats in future! The cat's physical and mental welfare is safeguarded at every stage of the test.

If all is still going well the dog is allowed off the lead, still muzzled, so that it can mooch round the room on its own. If all is calm the lead is put back on and the muzzle taken off. If the indications are good, the test ends here. Many dogs will give indications of being cat-friendly and will then suddenly change their minds at some stage in the test.

When you bring home a dog that is said to be cat-friendly you should repeat the whole cat-test exactly as it is explained here. If everything goes well

A surprising number of greyhounds live comfortably with cats, and a good re-homing charity will test to identify those that are cat-friendly.

you can continue to have the dog and cat in the same room together, but not unsupervised at first. I would spend time daily with the cat and dog in the same room with me before I thought of leaving them unsupervised, and I would always make sure the cat has a safe bolt-hole. You will be able to judge how things are progressing, and when to relax your guard.

Some dogs appear cat-friendly because they have never seen a cat before, and then they suddenly seem to realize that actually it is prey! Some dogs are frightened of a cat that has smacked them on the nose, and then one day when the cat is asleep decide to get their own back. Most cat-friendly dogs live very happily with cats for years, and will often interact with them in a loving way, sharing beds and food.

If you have a timid cat it may choose to live upstairs until it is used to the dog. No two dog/cat relationships are the same. It is possible to make some dogs that are not cat-friendly change their views, but it doesn't work with all dogs and it takes a long time, usually months, with the dog spending most of its time muzzled and on a lead.

It is cruel and unacceptable to try aversion collars for any training, and I would like to see them banned. The electric shock that the collar gives the dog raises his stress levels hugely. He may associate this with the cat, or he may become scared of something else entirely, possibly even you. Using the collar gives the dog such a shock initially that it seems to be working, but once your back is turned or the collar is off he may well want to get his own back on that cat!

TRAINING CLASSES

If you have decided to go to training classes with your dog, leave it a month or two until he has settled in and knows you as someone he can trust. Training classes are quite intimidating for a dog that has just come out of kennels, so let him get used to the big wide world first. Resist the idea of sending him away on his own to residential training kennels unless you can go too! Otherwise you won't know if he is being treated appropriately, and you will miss out on the fact that, often when you do get professional help, you find you will learn as much as the dog does.

AND FINALLY......

If you feel uncertain of anything during your first few days, do ring the rescue charity your dog came from and ask for advice. Rest assured that the majority of retired greyhounds settle down easily in the home and become a treasured member of the family for many years to come.

6 DAY-TO-DAY CARE OF YOUR GREYHOUND

Point three of the Greyhound Charter states that 'all greyhounds should be provided with suitable food and accommodation, and should have unrestricted access to fresh water'. Let's take time here to consider in detail not just what is suitable, but what is the best care you can provide for your new greyhound, and also how best you can help him to settle in.

DIET

Greyhounds do best on 'complete' food. This is a ready made-up meal that you can buy in small or large quantities at supermarkets and pet centres. There is no need to add anything else to this food, though you can add moisture (water) if you wish. These foods are formulated to provide a balanced diet, and to ensure your dog gets exactly what he needs. Dogs on complete diets must have access to water twenty-four hours a day. Note that the packs of dog food that are biscuit meal only, for mixing with cooked or tinned meat, are not suitable as a greyhound feed.

There is a huge variety of complete food on the market, and you need to find the one that suits your dog best. High protein diets are too rich for resting greyhounds, so look for a food that has not more than 20 per cent protein in its analysis. The analysis and ingredients should be displayed on the packet to help you choose. The ingredients on a good food will tell you exactly what meat it contains. If it just says 'meat derivatives' it could contain any waste product from meat production. Food with a high fibre content is more satisfying for energetic dogs.

The price of complete food varies hugely. The most expensive foods are usually very good quality, and the bonus with these is that there is very little waste so your dog produces very small, dry faeces. On cheaper foods you will find you need a bigger shovel! Note that food for working dogs carries no VAT, so if you can find a good quality working dog food with less than 20 per cent protein you will save yourself a great deal of money.

Be aware that sudden changes in diet will probably give your dog diarrhoea, and he may also suffer from that when he first experiences the changes that being in a new home will bring. Try to make any changes gradual by mixing in the new food with some of his old food for a few days.

If your dog becomes hyperactive or lethargic, or has minor stomach upsets, suspect that his diet is not suitable for him and gradually try something else. Give each trial at least three weeks to get a fair picture of whether it is working or not. Be prepared to spend time finding the ideal diet. Be aware that, just like us, some dogs do well on a diet for many years and then build up intolerance, so

Feeding guide diagram.

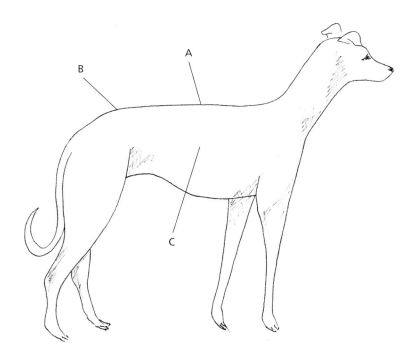

the fact that he has always been fine on a particular diet isn't a good reason for staying with it if it has become less suitable.

Having a small digestive system, greyhounds do best on two meals a day. As a rough guide the total daily intake for a small greyhound is about 350g (12oz), and for a large one about 450g (16oz), but like us, they vary individually and you need to keep an eye on your greyhound's condition and adjust the food accordingly.

Condition Score

A) You should be able to feel three vertebrae.
B) You should be able to feel, but not see, the hip bones on each side.
C) You should be able to see three ribs.

Feeding Guide

Your dog will need a raised food bowl, as deep-chested dogs find it difficult to eat off floor level. Your local pet shop should be able to provide a feed bowl and stand. You can also get a stand that holds water and feed bowls side by side; however, never be tempted to use this to feed two dogs side by side, as the bowls are placed very close together and this could risk an argument.

When your greyhound first comes out of racing he will have changed from a very rich racing greyhound diet to a resting greyhound diet; as a result his coat may have become dull, and he may be losing hair. To improve his coat you can give him oily fish twice a week. Sardines, pilchards or mackerel in oil is best (but not tuna because it can contain high

61

mercury levels which is not good for dogs). Just a dessertspoonful added to his meal will make a difference; alternatively you can give him evening primrose oil twice a week. Once he has become used to his resting diet his coat will regain its bloom.

Never exercise a dog on a full stomach, as this can cause a potentially serious illness called bloat. Always exercise either before you feed, or over an hour afterwards. (Note that when teaching recall it is best to exercise before you feed, while the dog is hungry.)

Please remember that dogs do not steal. 'Steal' is a word from our human vocabulary, and if you leave food where your dog can reach it, his instinctive reaction will be to mop it up.

THE RETIRED GREYHOUND AND FOOD ORIENTATION

A racing greyhound will have been kept down to racing weight during his racing career, when ideally you should be able to see all his ribs; he is therefore underweight compared with the domestic pet. In kennel life, every morsel of food that appears in a dog's kennel will be for him, so your greyhound can have no idea that any food left lying around in your kitchen is not his. If he has been one of the unlucky ones that have been abandoned before they found their way into a home, they will be very keen to eat any food left around as they may have faced starvation for some days, or even had to fight for their food.

Thus it may be that the dog you bring home thinks all food is his, or it may be one that thinks it must eat everything and anything as there may not be food tomorrow. Both situations may make the dog seem acquisitive and greedy, and if

this is not handled properly, aggressive behaviour may develop when there is food around, and this could have sad repercussions for both owner and dog.

Some Golden Food Rules
It is a good idea to institute some 'food rules' so that your dog, family members and visitors learn to co-exist safely with food:

- First of all, never leave food within reach, or leave the food waste-bin accessible for him to raid. And if he does get hold of food or raid the bin, don't be cross, as this will increase his concept of conflict over food: he wasn't being naughty, he has no concept of theft, and it is your fault. If he has taken something you don't want him to have, never try to grab it back because either he may defend it aggressively, or when he knows you want it he will enjoy not letting you have it and will turn it into a game, which you won't win! Distract him by calling him invitingly into another room for a treat, and then get someone to remove the object while he is in the other room, or shut him out while you return and remove it safely.
- When you are preparing food for yourself or the dog he may at first want to jump up at the worktop and try to snatch it. Don't get cross, simply position your body so that it blocks his access to the food and pushes him away. Keep blocking him, but don't speak to him or look at him, as that is confrontational. Be consistent about not giving him titbits when you are doing this.
- Initially keep everyone else in the family, especially children, away from him when you are preparing his food

and when he is eating, and never touch his food bowl while he is eating. Some people think it is clever to take the dog's bowl away while he is eating; they seem to think it makes him a 'safer' dog. In fact it could easily work the opposite way, and make him much more defensive of his food when other people are around. How would you feel if you were eating in a restaurant and someone took your food away? Such an action serves no real purpose and can create serious conflict.

- Don't make him 'sit' or 'wait' or do fancy tricks for his food: it means nothing to him, but just increases his stress levels – and why would you want to do that? Just say his name as you put his bowl down, and walk away.
- Initially don't eat snacks at his level. Sit to the table for food rather than snacking on the sofa, until he understands the message that your food is not for him. Don't feed him titbits at the table or give him your plates to lick, because that will confuse the message.

- Don't let children wander around with food or sweets, as this will make them vulnerable , and if you have a toddler using a high chair don't lift them down until spilled food has been cleared up.
- If your dog has a strong food orientation it is better to put these rules in place than to avoid the problem by excluding him when you are preparing food. If you exclude him he will never learn.

Some retired greyhounds take longer than others to learn that there will always be food for them tomorrow, and that they don't have to be opportunist about food. Other breeds of dog can be possessive about food too, even though they have not faced hunger in their lives. At least greyhounds have a good excuse for being food oriented, and happily once they know they are always going to be fed they will respect your food!

GROOMING

Greyhound coats are easy to look after.

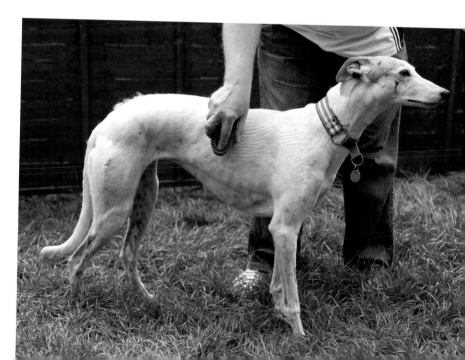

Use a soft brush or grooming mitt to groom a greyhound's short, soft coat.

Greyhounds are short-haired, and after a change of coat when they come out of racing they moult very little; only a soft brush or grooming mitt is needed for grooming. You will also need to trim your greyhound's claws regularly (*see* Chapter 7 Health Care).

Some greyhounds are happy for you to touch them all over, but others are very sensitive, especially round the ears and neck, or feet. You may find that if you grab at your greyhound's collar or play with its ears it will suddenly squeal. To get him used to being touched it is a good idea to 'paint' your greyhound regularly! By this I mean, imagine that your hand is a paintbrush and you are going to emulsion your dog and you mustn't miss anywhere. Start somewhere where he enjoys being stroked, then work towards a place where he is more sensitive until you stroke that area just once, then return to the place where he feels more comfortable about the procedure. If your greyhound becomes tense at any stage, go back to the more comfortable area. If you do this regularly he will soon become quite relaxed about you stroking him everywhere. This is really useful should your greyhound injure itself and need treatment in a sensitive spot.

EXERCISE

Two twenty-minute walks a day on the lead will give your greyhound enough basic exercise, especially if he has a garden to mooch around in. Greyhounds are surprisingly lazy, and are very happy to sleep for hours on end. However, he may require more mental stimulation, particularly if you are going to leave him for any length of time, and also if he is a young dog. Playing with another dog or playing some of the games described in Chapter 8 will help. If you can find an enclosed space where he can be let off the lead safely, this will help too, and you can use this opportunity to start working on recall. Don't be tempted to let him off the lead if his recall is not established, or the area is not safely enclosed; there is no need to take such a risk, and he will be fine with lead walking until the right moment.

It is worth looking on the internet for greyhound or sight hound playgroups. These are usually run by keen dog owners who get together and hire a safe venue such as an equine ménage for a few hours once a week. You can apply to take your dog along. The dogs are run free in small groups, wearing muzzles, and have a great time using up all their excess energy. The people running the playgroup put rules in place to keep all the dogs safe and to allow every dog to have a fair amount of exercise. Check that they have liability insurance and first aid cover before you join. And if you can't find one locally, consider starting one of your own!

WARMTH

Greyhounds are very thin skinned, and not made for our British weather. Consider the fact that they originally came from places with a warm climate, such as Egypt. It is not suitable for a greyhound to live outside in an unheated kennel or shed. Even in the home they can feel cold if the heat goes off at night. I don't believe in dressing up animals, but I do provide my greyhounds with a warm fleece at night in the winter, or when I take them on camping holidays. I also provide them with a warm, fleece-lined waterproof jacket when they are out

A contented greyhound will often lie on its back with its legs in the air.

mooching round the garden in the winter. Greyhounds hate to be wet and will often be very reluctant to go in the garden for a toilet visit if the weather is awful. Wearing a warm waterproof jacket outside often helps with toilet training for this reason.

BEDS

As well as being thin-coated, greyhounds are bony so they need thick, soft bedding such as that recommended in Chapter 3. As with all dogs, the positioning of the bed is important, too. No dog likes to sleep in a draughty passageway with people clambering past him all the time. It is also important that the dog has his bed in a place he can call his own so that he can retreat to it if he feels stressed or uncomfortable. We should respect this space. When he retires to his bed for some peace and quiet it is not fair for us to invade it. Dogs like to have their backs to the wall, and a niche or alcove is really cosy for them. For all these reasons it is worth spending some thought on finding a really cosy space for their bed.

Keeping your greyhound warm and comfortable will make him content, and if he is contented, you will be contented too!

7 HEALTH CARE

VACCINATIONS

Your retired greyhound should have been vaccinated against diseases such as distemper, hard pad, parvovirus and leptospirosis. All of these diseases are potential killers and it is heartbreaking to watch an unvaccinated dog die because its owners did not act responsibly in getting it vaccinated. A booster will need to be given every year to continue this protection. Your rescue charity should provide you with your new dog's vaccination record card, in which the vet will record all subsequent booster vaccinations, and you will be required to keep this up to date. If you home a greyhound that has not been vaccinated it is essential that you get this done as soon as possible to keep him healthy. If you go on holiday and want to put your dog in kennels he will not be allowed into the kennels unless his vaccinations are up to date. Some kennels require an extra protection against kennel cough too, which is given as an intra-nasal vaccine. It is best to enquire about this when booking a dog's stay in kennels so that you have time to get it done.

TEETH

Greyhounds often get a heavy deposit of tartar on their teeth, which makes their

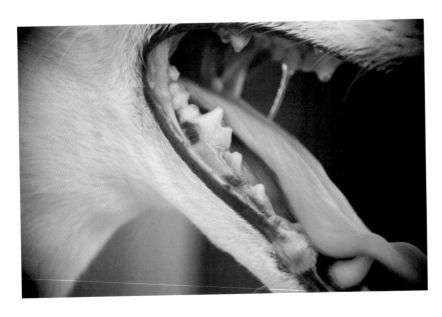

This dog's top teeth and the canine tooth in his lower jaw have tartar.

An example of clean greyhound teeth with no tartar. Daily dental sticks will help keep them clean.

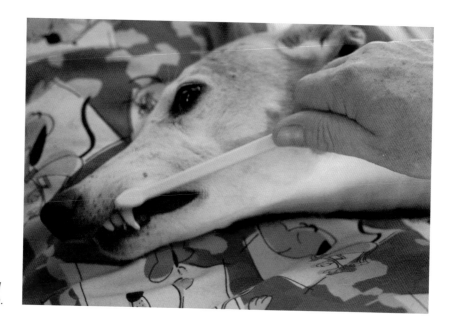

You can use a brush and special dog toothpaste to keep your greyhound's teeth clean and his breath fresh.

breath smell dreadful! Good rescue charities will have asked their vet to check the dog's teeth before it is homed, and if necessary to carry out some dental work. This is usually done under general anaesthetic, and if your dog's teeth are really bad you will need to follow this route.

As a matter of routine it is a good idea to try to keep the teeth tartar free by providing good quality dental sticks for your dog to chew on a daily basis, and a dental bone once a week. Most large supermarkets stock these. If you can do this, your dog will probably never need to have any dental work done. Greyhounds do not respond well to anaesthetic, so if you can keep your dog's teeth clean this way it is cheaper and safer. You can also buy meaty-tasting, special dog toothpaste from your vet, and clean your dog's teeth daily. Never use human toothpaste; it is usually too strong for dogs and contains chlorine, which may give the dog an upset stomach.

GREYHOUNDS AND ANAESTHETICS

Please be aware that, having a different metabolism from other breeds of dog, greyhounds experience difficulty in metabolizing some anaesthetics. If your greyhound is booked in for an operation you will need to check that the vet is aware of greyhound problems with anaesthesia. These dogs have a low level of body fat and are therefore susceptible to hypothermia when recovering from sedatives or general anaesthetics.

NEUTERING

All good rescue charities will ensure that their greyhounds are neutered before they are homed. If you offer a home to a greyhound that is not neutered, whether it is male or female, it is important to get this done as soon as possible. The reason there are so many retired greyhounds available for adoption is because far too many are bred. We certainly don't want more homeless dogs produced through careless greyhound breeding. Owning a greyhound that has not been neutered is not easy. When a bitch comes in season she has to be kept indoors otherwise all the male dogs in the area will get to know her condition and will camp on your doorstep. Equally the bitch herself, when she comes in season, succumbs to the instinctive urge to go and find a mate, so you cannot expect her to co-operate by choosing to stay at home if she can possibly find a way out. Similarly an entire dog will be very aware of bitches in season and will want to go to them; furthermore he will also exhibit all sorts of masculine behaviour that you would prefer to be without. It therefore really is urgent that your new greyhound is neutered.

FLEAS, TICKS AND MITES

All dogs can be victim to these parasites. The advantage of a greyhound is that you can see if it has them more easily than you can on a long-coated dog. Ticks can carry Lyme's disease, which can also affect humans. Dogs usually pick them up when they are running through long grass, gorse or heather where wild animals have grazed. The ticks drop on to the dog and attach themselves by the mouthpart, sucking the dog's blood till they swell and are clearly seen. Remove the tick straightaway by twisting gently so that it doesn't leave its mouthparts in the dog. Symptoms of Lyme disease are

Use a proper preparation from your vet for flea control.

loss of appetite, fever, lethargy and sometimes lameness, but these may not become evident until months after the tick bite occurred.

Fleas sometimes cause an unsightly skin allergy, as do the mites that dogs pick up from foxes – and these can spread fox mange. If you notice your dog itching you need to act quickly to stop the infestation spreading. The preparations you can buy in supermarkets are generally not strong enough to deal with the problem, and you really need to get a proper medication from the vet to be fully effective. A good preparation will start killing fleas immediately, but will take about a fortnight to rid the dog of fox mites. If your dog is still scratching and developing bald patches after treatment he may

have developed an allergy to the parasite and will need further veterinary care to get over it. He won't recover on his own, and the situation will worsen rapidly if he is not given treatment.

WORMS

These are internal parasites that also need to be treated. A dog with worms will have a dull coat and look undernourished; however, it is better to treat for worms before the dog reaches this stage. Worm treatment that you can buy over the counter or in supermarkets is rarely effective, and you will need to go to your vet for the proper medication and for advice on how often to worm your dog to keep it parasite free.

Racing circuits are all counter clockwise, which may put considerable strain on the wrist and toe joints, causing arthritis in later life. (Photo provided by Nick Guise-Smith www.mirrorboxstudios.co.uk)

INJURIES

The circuits on which greyhounds race are always anti-clockwise, and the centrifugal forces of the sharp bends put great strain on the dogs' wrist joints and toes. Many collide or fall at terrific speed, and injuries are bound to occur, which prevent them from continuing their racing career. They do not stop the retired greyhound living a full and happy life as a domestic pet, but be aware that as a result he may suffer with arthritis later on in his life.

Many trainers swim their injured dogs to help them recover, as a form of exer-

Greyhounds often have bald patches on their thighs.

cise that is not weight-bearing on their limbs. There are pet centres where you can take a dog that has injured a limb privately for this hydrotherapy treatment, which often brings excellent results. Although greyhounds will not usually go for a swim by choice when they encounter water in the course of a walk, they are perfectly able to do so;

Hydrotherapy clinics offer swimming as a non weight-bearing exercise for dogs with injuries.

moreover the water in the hydrotherapy bath is warm, which appeals to them more.

Sometimes greyhounds wag their tails so hard in kennels that they damage them against the walls. Your new greyhound may have a split tail when it arrives, but it will soon repair once it is away from kennel walls.

THE COAT AND SKIN

Greyhounds often have bald patches on their thighs, especially if bedding has been thin in their racing kennels; however, living in a home where the bedding is soft and the feeding good will help to improve the situation. Refer to the chapter on feeding if your greyhound has bald patches. Remember, too, that the greyhound pelt is thin, and if greyhounds run excitedly through brambles and fences, or play 'nip and tuck' with other dogs, their pelts will tear easily. My greyhound pup once had to have fourteen stitches when a game with my other dog became too enthusiastic. I didn't blame the other dog and think that she should be re-homed or put down, as some people would; the two were the best of friends, and there was no malice: it was simply a game that went too far.

PROBLEMS IN THE FEET

A greyhound's claws need regular trimming. If they are neglected the claws will curl under the dog's feet, digging into the pads and making it walk awkwardly, often causing further problems. You can buy dog claw clippers in pet shops, but before you attempt to do the job yourself it is a good idea to learn from your vet how to do it properly.

Racing greyhounds spend much of their time exercising on grass and sand tracks, so their feet may be quite soft when they retire. Beware of walking them too much on hard ground initially or they will get sore feet. You can help harden their feet by massaging them with surgical spirit daily for two weeks.

Problems with Corns

Occasionally some greyhounds get corns in their feet. If your greyhound is lame but you can see no reason for it, a corn may be developing. Check if the dog can walk better on soft ground: this will give you a clearer indication of whether it might be a corn. A few weeks after the onset of lameness you will be able to see a circular patch of hard skin on the pad.

Vets are still seeking solutions to this problem of corns, which is rare in other breeds of dog. Web sites abound with advice on many types of preparation that are supposed to remove corns, but I have never had success with any of them. Surgical removal is a good option, but occasionally the corns return soon afterwards and further surgery is needed. Always look for a specialist greyhound vet to carry out this procedure. It is well worth using surgery on a young dog; with an old dog management may be a better option.

Corns can be treated using silver (and it must be silver) duct tape. Cut a small piece exactly the size of the corn and stick it on the corn, not on the healthy pad tissue. Keep replacing it when it falls off.

As the corn softens it will adhere better. After about two weeks you will be able to get a fingernail behind the edge of the corn. Soak the dog's foot in warm water for ten minutes, and then you will find you can painlessly remove the corn – or a large chunk of it. Sometimes if the corn is small you can remove it for good this way. Large, deep corns can't be removed this way, but they can be managed. There are many types of dog boot you can buy to help your dog walk more comfortably on hard surfaces if it has corns, or after corn surgery, to prevent them recurring.

BLOAT/TORSION/POISONING

Avoid exercising your dog straight after its meal, and don't allow him access to unsuitable human food, or the rubbish

It is a good idea to get the vet to show you how to clip your greyhound's nails properly.

On the front left pad you can see a small circle of hard skin. This is a corn.

bin. All these scenarios can cause bloat, where the stomach is unnaturally distended because it is full of food and gas; this can lead to torsion, where the stomach becomes twisted. The symptoms are restlessness, drooling, abdominal pain and retching. Bloat and torsion are generally the result of mismanagement.

This condition is an emergency – because a dog that has bloat and torsion has a slim chance of recovering. Greyhounds especially move very fast at exercise, twisting and turning at speed, and it is therefore really important to follow the 'no exercise on a full stomach' rule.

At Christmas vets often see this problem, or poisoning as a result of dogs being able to help themselves to Christmas cakes or boxes of chocolates that have been left within their reach. It is so easy in all the excitement to forget to take the usual care, and if you lose your

dog because of this, it will surely ruin your festive season.

Human foods that are poisonous to dogs include chocolate, grapes, raisins, coffee, cocoa, onions, mushrooms, walnuts, apricot and peach stones and any part of an avocado.

Light Stomach Upsets

If your dog seems a little under the weather and his stools are runny or he is sick, it is best to let him miss a meal and at the next meal feed a light diet such as cooked chicken and rice. Make sure he still has access to clean water. This will give his tummy time to sort itself out. If the symptoms worsen or persist for more than a day or two he should be taken to the vet.

This light diet is also good for a dog that is recovering from surgery or other illness.

BEREAVEMENT

If you have more that one dog and one of them dies, the other may well feel a sense of bereavement. I let my other dogs see and smell the body because I think it gives them a sense of understanding that the other dog has 'gone', and generally they cope with it well. The only time I didn't show my border collie the other dog's body he was restless for some days and kept wandering off – possibly to look for his friend. He then became agoraphobic about going out for a walk. This may have been a coincidence, but since then I have always kept to my usual rule, and subsequently any bereaved dogs have not developed such problems.

THE FINAL DAYS

We all say how easy it would be if our elderly canine companion were just to slip away in his sleep one night. Sadly this rarely happens, and often we are in the position of having to decide whether euthanasia is the last resort to ease his pain and distress. This is your own personal decision. No one will tell you to make it, but your vet will help you to reach it by discussing the alternatives and by explaining how much your dog may be suffering. You will know when it is time.

To most of us the loss of our dog is incredibly distressing. Some people feel guilty because they are as distressed about losing a family pet as they are about any other family member. But why shouldn't we feel that way? Our pet was a long-standing and much loved member of our family, and as valued as every other member, so we are quite within our rights to grieve.

Your vet will also help you to reach a decision about whether your pet should be buried or cremated. You can spread the ashes in his favourite place in the garden, and it is often very comforting to know he is still there.

Many animal owners find comfort from the beautiful poem *Rainbow Bridge* by Paul C. Dahm, in which he conceives of dying as running across the Rainbow Bridge that links Earth and Heaven; here, pets will meet other past companions and will run free until they are reunited with their owners again. Writing this I am reminded of the wonderful canine friends who have been part of my life.

Run the Rainbow Bridge,
my friends,
and run free …

OPPOSITE: Run to the rainbow bridge my friends and run free…

8 GAMES

When greyhounds first retire from racing their knowledge of toys and games is limited, or in some cases non-existent. You can buy your dogs the most beautiful toy in the world, but it is an inanimate object as far as the dog is concerned.

When greyhounds are trained to chase the lure, the reward they get determines what kind of toy they might see as interesting. Some dogs are rewarded by having a soft toy thrown to them. As it is thrown it is moving, so it suddenly becomes interesting; also the trainer is pleased, and encourages the dog to play with his reward by calling excitedly to him. Some trainers use a carrier bag with treats in, and the dog rips up the bag to get at the treats. This explains why some greyhounds have a soft toy fetish and some have a carrier bag fetish!

It is not worth buying expensive soft toys for greyhounds that have played with toys as a reward for chasing the lure. Most will enjoy ripping them up, which for a greyhound is a rewarding pastime, so I usually buy cheap toys from charity shops; I am careful to check there are no dangerous parts before giving them to my dogs. If your greyhound investigates your shopping excitedly when you come in the door it is obvious that his reward for chasing the lure has been a bag of food, so be careful about leaving shopping lying around.

PLAYING WITH A TOY

Some greyhounds have no interest in toys at all and need to be introduced to the concept of playing. Play will give your dog exercise and relieve any frustration, particularly while he is not ready to be let off the lead.

Many greyhounds absolutely love soft toys.

Some greyhounds enjoy a tug of war with a toy, but don't feel you have to win. Give it a little tug and then let it go.

If a dog starts off by showing no interest at all in a toy, it is up to you to make that toy interesting. Choose a moment when the dog is awake and mooching around looking for something to do. Hold the toy in one hand, and keep showing it to the dog, then moving it behind your back saying excitedly something like 'Where's it gone?'. Move it quickly with sharp movements. A squeaky toy often gets a more interested response. As soon as the dog makes an interested move towards it, praise him and raise the excitement level in your voice. He may follow it when you put it behind you, or he may try to get hold of it.

Reward him by chucking it in the air and letting him get it. Don't chuck it far away – he is not interested enough yet to make too much effort to get it. If he picks it up and runs with it, encourage him. Try having a little tug of war. In the old days of behaviour work we were told never to have a tug of war with a dog unless you could win because you 'must be the master'. But consider this: if you had a tug of war with your Dad when you were younger, and your Dad let you win, would you suddenly think less of him and that he wasn't fit to be a dad? No, you would just enjoy the game, and come back for more!

With a dog that is really slow to take interest in the toy, try giving him a treat immediately he takes notice of it by looking at it or touching it with his nose. This is not so easy, because you should be trying to make the toy the reward rather than the treat, and if you are not instant with the treat, the message is lost.

Alongside getting your dog interested in toys, you need to be developing a 'game over' technique so that you can stop the game and take away the toy safely. After you have built up interest in the toy, if you leave it lying around it becomes an inanimate object again, which undoes all your hard work. Have a treat in your pocket which you can exchange for the toy to finish the game, and put the toy away until next time. You can use a key word to end the game as you give the treat. At first the dog may follow you, jumping up for the toy, but turn away and ignore him; if you give in, he will not respect the 'game over' signal.

Spend some time finding out what is your dog's favourite reward now that he has been introduced to toys. Is it still treats, or is it a particular toy? It is always useful to know if there is something that will take your dog's interest above all else (though maybe not next door's cat – but above most other things).

Now he is ready to learn some games. 'See-stalk-chase-grab bite-kill bite' is the sequence that gives the greyhound 'job satisfaction'. But don't worry, there is not going to be any killing; we are simply going to remodel the 'kill' part into another reward!

The purpose of these games is to exercise your dog mentally and physically.

TUG OF WAR

This is easy, but go gently – it is not a battle. There is no place for hanging on so tightly that you are swinging a greyhound by its teeth; just have a little tug and then let go. Your dog will probably rush off excitedly round the garden with his prize, and will then run back close to you inviting you to have another go. Give the toy another little tug and off he will go again! He is doing the exercise, you are just reinforcing the stimulus. In a dog to dog tug of war the more confident dog usually gets the prize and carries it round like a trophy and this helps Behaviourists to identify the more confident dog. But your dog knows you are not a dog. He knows this is just a game. After the first tug you may not actually need to touch the toy again. Just put your hand out to try and touch the toy as he goes past, and this is enough to keep him playing for ages. You don't even need to get out of your deck chair. However your lawn will never be the same again!

HIDE AND SEEK

You need two people to establish this indoor or outdoor game, one to hide, and one to hold the dog on the lead. The first time you hide, choose a fairly simple place, building up to more difficult places as he gets more interested in the game. The hider needs to have the dog's favourite reward ready – either a treat or a soft toy for when he finds you. The person holding the dog now encourages him by using an exciting voice. What you say doesn't matter, just 'Where is she?' will do. The person hiding then calls the dog encouragingly. The person holding the dog runs with him to find the person hiding, and the dog gets an immediate reward to satisfy the 'kill' bit of the deal. Some dogs take to the game straightaway, and some go along with it reluctantly, but once they understand that there is a reward involved they begin to enjoy it, and then you can dispense with the lead.

Many dogs enjoy the game so much that the reward is in finding you and the treat is no longer needed You can move on to playing it without anyone holding the dog if you can just creep off and hide when he isn't looking. The more exciting you make the game, the more exciting it will be for the dog; however, you have to be the one who gives the game credibility.

HUNT THE TREAT

This game is very similar to hide and seek. Hide the treat somewhere simple at first, such as behind the sofa. The smellier the treat is, the better: tripe sticks are good for this. Let the dog smell the hand that has held the treat, and then using an excited voice to urge your dog to start looking, run round the house saying something like, 'Where is it?' pointing out places where it might be. Make it easy at first, and increase the level of difficulty as the dog gets more used to the game. Aim to progress to the point where you can go out in the garden to hide a few treats, and then let your dog take himself off on his treat hunt. If he likes digging, bury some in a small sand-pit!

FETCH

Retrieving is not a greyhound's strong point. He likes the stalk, the chase and the kill, but then for him the game is over. Why on earth should he fetch the kill for you? So this needs perseverance. Get him excited in the toy by giving it credibility, then toss it into the air – though not too far, as greyhounds are lazy dogs. If he picks it up and runs with it he will circle round to invite you to join his game. Don't step forwards, but crouch

down with a big, obvious treat in your hand, and offer him a swap. If he takes it, let him finish eating it, then offer him another throw. And repeat the procedure. Don't expect an instant return yet, and wait till he is already coming towards you before offering the swap. Keep it short.

After two or three goes most greyhounds will be looking for a place to snooze, and you will want to end the game before he decides it is boring. Try and do a little of this every day and he will learn fetch, maybe not the instant fetch that a gundog will give you, but enough of a fetch that you can use it to give him some exercise.

DOUBLE FETCH

This sounds harder than the 'fetch', but actually it is much easier, and is useful if you can't be bothered to teach the proper 'fetch'. Get him interested in a toy, and then throw it. When he picks it up and is running round, as he comes towards you introduce another toy, wave it around to make it interesting, and then throw it. Hopefully he will drop the first toy in his eagerness to get the second. Now you've got the first toy back ready to throw next time he comes round.

POTS

Put a plastic plant pot down on the floor and let your dog see you put a treat under it. Hold the pot over the treat and let the dog investigate. He will go through his repertoire of how to get the treat. The moment he touches the pot with his nose, lift the pot up and allow him to have the treat. When he understands that touching the pot with his

Safe Flight (Foxy) enjoying the plant-pot game.

nose gets him the treat, introduce two pots but one treat, and allow him the treat when he touches the correct pot. Add another pot. When the game is well established, try moving the pots around – though not too much, because he might decide to go off for a snooze if it gets too difficult.

A SETTLED DOG

Greyhounds are simple to please. For instance my friend's greyhound loves it if you blow at him; he then runs a mad circuit round the garden and comes back for another blow. Most greyhounds will play by just having a 'funny five minutes', where they decide to dash off madly in all directions just for the fun of it. I usually stand by a tree on these occasions, otherwise you can get knocked over like a skittle as they go by.

If your greyhound has had a good walk and a good play in the garden he is much more likely to settle happily if you have to leave him.

Many problem dogs of all breeds are suffering from the frustration of a life that doesn't allow them to express their natural feelings. The needs that their breed characteristics demand haven't been met. If your dog is manic and demanding, think to yourself – in his working life what would he have been doing on a daily basis that he is not getting the chance to do now? Then find a way of replicating that behaviour in a game to relieve his frustration, and you will have a much more settled dog.

9 PROBLEM-SOLVING

I have avoided calling this chapter 'Behavioural Problems' because that implies that the fault always lies with the dog. Nor do I want to imply that the fault lies with the human. Problems happen when the human and the dog can't communicate well, and considering that they 'speak' entirely different languages, it is hardly surprising when things go wrong.

Humans have a broad vocabulary of spoken language; we also have a broad vocabulary of body language, though we are not always so good at reading and interpreting that. Dogs communicate largely by body language. Is that a surprise? If they communicated mostly by vocal language they would be yipping and yapping all the time and we would soon get fed up with that. I wonder if they get fed up with our constant chatter.

We want our dogs to be the perfect pet. We want them to follow us to heel, to sleep quietly all night, behave perfectly on and off the lead ignoring all other stimuli, understand the monetary value of items in the house (for example 'I will be more angry if you eat the remote control than if you eat an old newspaper'), and to not stand on the furniture to get a better view. The list is endless.

All our dogs want is food, water, shelter, safety, freedom to explore, freedom to respond to exciting stimuli such as the cat next door, freedom to chew for comfort, the opportunity to explode with excitement and play, and freedom to express an opinion.

So our list of wants is entirely different from those of our dogs. No wonder we sometimes don't see eye to eye.

COMMUNICATING WITH YOUR DOG

How does a dog express an opinion? A positive opinion – for example 'I'm happy we are going for a walk' – leads to an explosion of leaping and barking and twirling, which may make his owner cross if it is difficult to put the lead on. A negative opinion – such as 'I don't want you to sit on my bed with me just now because I want peace and quiet' – is expressed by stillness, and an intense look in the eye. This is a warning, and if you insist on staying on the dog's bed, what can he do next to tell you his message? Growl. And if you are still there, he has only one way left of getting the message across, and that is to snap – you have given him no other choice. The next step will be a bite. He has told you his opinion and he has given you three chances to listen.

What is the human response? To say the dog is dangerous and to have him euthanased for expressing an opinion in the only way he knows. Is that fair?

A dog is a dog, his language is his heritage, and his heritage is wild animal.

We cannot change him into a human, and why would we want to? If you can learn to communicate with your dog well by understanding his language, you will have a great partnership. Dogs are not born evil or nasty; generally speaking they want to please (goodness knows why), but they don't know how. When you ask a dog to do something, the question in his mind is 'What's in it for me?' If you give him the right answer you will get what you want.

RESEARCH INTO BEHAVIOUR

Behaviour work with animals has come a long way in the last fifty years. Many of us did things the way we did because that is the way our parents did it, and what was good enough for them was good enough for us, so we don't progress, or consider there might be a better way. Now the behaviour work we do is based on research, so often we know something we do will work, and we know why. At first, research into dog behaviour was based on wolf packs living in captivity. We thought that dogs were wolves in dogs' clothing, and that the pack (our family and dogs) needed to be organized like a pack with Mr and Mrs Owner at the top and the dogs at the bottom.

However, after further research there appeared to be two major flaws in this thinking. The first was that wolf packs in the wild were found not to have such a hierarchical existence as we had previously thought, and in fact operated in family groups similar to our own. The second was that dogs did not descend directly from the predecessors of our modern-day wolves, but developed alongside as a subspecies that elected to live on the periphery of human settlements, surviving as scavengers. In fact although a group of dogs may sometimes hunt together in a pack (especially hounds), they don't live as packs, or have a hierarchical lifestyle, and are often absolutely hopeless at living wild. (Why are strays always so thin?)

Within a group of dogs there are those who are more confident in certain situations than others, just as in human groups, but it doesn't mean that they are totally in charge. One of the worst words in the English language ever associated with dogs was 'dominance'. Dogs are not 'dominant': they don't think they are above people and other dogs, and leading the pack – they are just dogs. A pushy dog might be rather bad mannered but we can do something about that, and a possessive dog might be grumpy but we can do something about that too – but I can assure you that dogs are not making a bid to take over the world. The 'D' word will not therefore be used again in this book, and it has no place in a dog's world.

So what problems might we meet with our retired greyhounds, and what can we do about them? Most dogs of any breed develop unwanted behaviour because they feel frustrated, when something in their lifestyle doesn't fit their needs. So first we need to look at breed characteristics. Your new dog is not a German Shepherd so it is unlikely that there will be issues concerning guarding or defending territory. Nor is it a Border Collie so it is unlikely to be energetically rounding up the whole family and dashing in to nip the heels of the slow ones! The point I am making here is that different dogs have been selectively bred for different purposes. A greyhound will usually exhibit greyhound-related problems, but as a breed they have no more problems than other breeds, and in most cases far fewer.

Greyhounds love to use their excellent sight to locate prey, then chase it, catch it and kill it. This is what they are and what they do, so this behaviour gives them a huge buzz. They may be retired, but they still have that urge, and it is unfair to expect them to suddenly lose it. However, we can make opportunities daily for them to get that buzz by playing 'chase and hunt' games, and this is why I have included a whole chapter on games in this book. A greyhound that is physically tired will settle down for a lazy day, but one that is mentally satisfied will settle far better. Moreover many problems will disappear altogether if your dog is getting the right sort of stimulating play for his breed characteristics.

The following is a catalogue of problems that might arise, and not necessarily just in greyhounds.

UNSUCCESSFUL TOILET TRAINING

Nine times out of ten if a dog persists in 'performing' in the house it is probably because he doesn't clearly understand what you want. In Chapter 4, The First Few Days, a start was made on toilet training. If you were able to work hard at this during his first week of homing the dog would understand what you want, but if you had to go out to work some days and only followed the advice spasmodically, the dog won't have understood. Take a weekend when you promise yourself that you are going to concentrate on helping the dog understand. Remember, never get cross: just anticipate when he needs to go, get him outside in time, and reward him immediately. If he has soiled in the house you need to clean it with a special pet toilet remover that will take away the smell. You can get this in most pet shops. If you use ordinary household cleaner, *you* may not be able to smell it any more, but the dog can, and it is almost shouting at him 'This is a toilet, you used it before, use it again!'

If he is still having trouble, ask the vet to have a look at him and see if there is anything wrong. If the vet gives an all clear, consider *when* the dog does it. Is it while you are out? If so, maybe he is finding the separation difficult, and needs work on separation anxiety, which will be covered later in this chapter.

Does he only do it at night? In which case did you go out with him for his last visit to the garden before bedtime to make sure he *did* go and do what you want? If not, he may just have hung about shivering outside the back door till you let him in again – after all, how does he know it is his last chance? If he does it at night only, it may be that he is cold and needs a fleece, or it may be that his meal needs to be dished up earlier to give it time to go through his digestive system *before* bedtime.

If he soils in strange places, such as on your bed, he is probably finding somewhere where he feels safe to do it because he knows you disapprove of the other places he has used. That is why it is important not to get cross, particularly as he may have done it hours before you find it and has forgotten all about it. He will have no idea why you are cross, and will probably creep away looking very upset because he senses you are grumpy with him for some reason. This is when people say that the dog 'knows he has done wrong' because he is creeping off with a 'guilty' look on his face. He is in fact creeping off looking worried in response to the signals you are giving off. If he knew it was wrong, why would he have done it? Dogs are not spiteful.

If your dog is unable to go through the night – if he wakes you up in the night by howling, or barking, or scratching the door – it may be that he just wants your company and knows that if he makes enough noise he will get what he wants. Try to avoid this situation by giving some thought as to why he is wide awake in the night so you can prevent the problem arising. Remember, for us 'the darkest hour is just before dawn': that is when we feel at our lowest ebb, and I think dogs may feel the same. Ask yourself the following questions:

- Is he cold? Put a fleece on at night.
- Is he scared? Leave a little nightlight on and maybe a quiet radio.
- Did something outside wake him up? Make sure the curtains are closed, and if his wakefulness is always at the same time every night, investigate what might be disturbing him.
- Does he need to relieve himself? Once you have been disturbed in the early hours or have woken up feeling cold, a visit to the loo is the inevitable next step, and maybe he feels the same.
- Did he really spend his last night let out wisely, or did he just mooch round outside the door hoping to be let in quickly because it was cold outside? Go with him and make sure he does perform before he comes back in. Greyhounds do have small digestive systems, and some find it difficult to go through a long night without a toilet visit.
- If you put water on his evening feed he is less likely to guzzle at the water bowl in the evening, and this often makes a big difference to his ability to

go through the night without a toilet stop. Taking him out in the garden more than once in the evening will help, as getting up and going out makes him more likely to offload before bedtime.

FEAR AGGRESSION

Many people think that dogs that growl and snap at strangers or other dogs are just nasty. However, they nearly always behave like this out of fear. Consider two young lads going on a bank raid: they have guns. One is confident, he has done this before, and it gives him a buzz – he feels in control of events. The other is scared, he is following his friend's lead, but he is not at all sure he can cope with this, even if he is putting on a brave face to impress his friend. Who is the one most likely to pull the trigger? It is therefore the fearful dog, not the confident dog, who is most likely to bite.

Greyhounds have often missed out on socialization with other breeds of dog, and some breeds have body language that is very difficult to read. They have stumpy tails and floppy ears so the signals they give off are like nothing a greyhound has ever seen before. Border collies are particularly intimidating because they have that hard, confrontational eye that they use to single out sheep from the flock!

Avoid introducing your greyhound to other dogs by allowing him to go forwards in front of you, because that is putting him in the front line. All dogs face potential problems by using freeze, flight and, as a last resort, fight. When your greyhound sees another dog he may freeze for a second; if he still feels scared, the next choice would be flight – but he is on the lead so flight is not available, therefore fight is the remaining option. This is when a scared dog will start barking and growling and leaping, to make himself look big and to 'psych' himself up. If you start shouting and jerking the lead you are joining in and giving him back-up – so now he feels even braver!

There were two moments in this scenario when you could have helped him. First, the moment he froze you could have stepped between him and the other dog, or silently moved him to the other side of you – whichever is easiest. Second, you could keep on walking either past, or away from, the other dog so that you are providing the flight option. It may take quite a few encounters before he understands that you can help him, so he may well still be 'kicking off' as you lead him away. If you keep his muzzle on while you walk him until you have solved this problem you will deal with it with far more confidence.

Always have a treat ready, and the first time you walk him past or away from another dog without him kicking off, praise him and slip him a treat immediately (if you use the basket-type muzzle it is easy to slip a long, thin treat in through the side). Continue doing this at every positive encounter until he has realized that looking to you for a treat is far more fun than worrying about another dog. Your own body language is really important: walk tall, appear confident, be calm and make no fuss. You are a sort of rôle model.

For dogs that do find the outside world a challenging place, keep the walks short but frequent, building up to more demanding excursions gradually. If your dog is suddenly frightened by something, go back a stage to a previous walk he was confident with, and build up slowly again. Never try to reassure him by comforting him; dogs do not understand the concept of sympathy, and you will only be confirming his belief that he is right to be scared.

Looking back at the bank raid scenario, if you have a dog that is nervous with people and they invade his space, he may feel the need to 'pull the trigger'. However, he will be fine if they will only leave him alone. While he is learning that the big wide world is not such a frightening place, ask visitors and people you encounter in the street not to look at him or greet him, but to completely ignore him and allow him to make all the first moves. Don't encourage him to go to people he doesn't know: he will, when he feels ready. Never crowd him or corner him; it is better to invite him into your space for a cuddle rather than going to him, so that he can walk away if he can't cope.

SEPARATION ANXIETY

Some dogs – of any breed – just do not cope well with being left at home alone. If you come back to a soiled carpet, or chewed furniture, or irate neighbours who have been deafened by your dog crying, please resist the urge to get cross with him. He behaved like this because he couldn't cope, and negative action will ensure that he will be even more stressed the next time you leave him, and the results will be worse.

It is to your advantage that racing greyhounds have often spent hours alone in kennels and do not expect day-long entertainment from humans, so they are less likely to suffer from separation anxiety than other breeds. You can deal with this problem initially by treating the symptoms, which is a stop-gap solution but will take the immediate pressure off

If you come home to a mess, resist the urge to be cross: the dog may have chewed because he was bored or stressed, and if you are angry he will be even more stressed next time you leave him.

you. When you go out, put the dog in a 'damage limitation zone', such as an indoor kennel or a utility room. Provide him with toys, or better still a kong stuffed with treats, and leave the radio on, turned down low. However, if the problem is deep-rooted he will ignore his treats and toys and may still cry. Never use your damage limitation zone as a punishment, as that will defeat the object. Your dog needs to feel that this place where you have chosen to leave him is the best place in the world to be: warm, safe, cosy and interesting.

Nevertheless you still need to look at the underlying problem, which may be that he is suffering from loneliness, or that he is bored. If he is lonely, and if another dog for company is out of the question, use the damage limitation zone, but also think about the way you are going to enter and leave the house. Make no fuss when you leave him, just pick up your keys and walk out. Say nothing. When you come back in, do the same: ignore him completely until he relaxes – yawns, stretches, blinks or lies down – then reward him by making a fuss of him. If you fuss him and talk to him before you go, he will pick up the feeling that you are concerned and this will add to his stress. Do consider getting him a settled companion; to my mind two greyhounds are even easier than one.

If it is boredom that is causing the problem, make sure he is physically and mentally satisfied before you go. A walk is not enough: he needs to play a 'seek, chase, catch, kill' game, too.

The best way of all to deal with all of this is to avoid the problem ever starting in the first place. This means an investment of your time, but it is so worthwhile. From day one, build up separation in small steps. Pop out of the room and shut the door behind you. Wait silently until he stops fussing for a few seconds, and then go straight in and reward him. A little later repeat it for a bit longer, and keep doing this until he understands that you will come back, but only if he waits quietly. Now build up to leaving the house for a few minutes, and gradually lengthen the time you are away. Never come back in if he is making a fuss: always wait until it is quiet, and then go in and give immediate praise. If there is soiling or damage, do *not* make a fuss. If you are calm he will learn from you. (Remember that you need to use a proper pet stain remover to stop your dog thinking the last place he soiled is a public loo!)

It is difficult to be calm when the dog has made a mess or chewed something. They chew for comfort, and often the damage has been done the minute after you leave, so if you come back and get cross hours later your dog has absolutely no idea what you are talking about. Furthermore if he looks shifty, it is not guilt: dogs do not have an understanding of guilt, he may just be responding to the unhappy signals you are giving off. Consider this: if a dog knows what guilt is, he would know he was doing wrong. So what would be his reason for deliberately doing wrong? Spite, or sulking because you have slighted him in some way? No, I don't think dogs are as complex as that. That is why we like

them, because they give us unconditional affection. If dogs were that clever *they* would be the ones running the world!

DEFENDING POSSESSIONS

Occasionally dogs will fiercely defend what they regard as their possessions, though this is more usual in a guarding breed such as a German Shepherd; nevertheless, sometimes a greyhound will do this.

Many greyhounds love to have something special of their own to take to bed with them. They do love soft toys, especially as these will have been used as a reward for chasing the lure when they were in training – but they can be possessive about them. Moreover as a hunting dog it is natural for the greyhound to catch his prey and then stand over it.

They also don't know at first which are their toys and which are yours. What is the difference between a piece of rawhide and the TV remote control? What is the difference between a soft toy and your slippers? The difference is that he has seen you use and play with the remote control and the slippers, so you

As a hunting dog it is natural for a greyhound to catch his prey and then stand guard over it, even if it is only a soft toy.

have given them validity! Better still, when he grabs hold of them you often give chase and clearly want them back, so the game is on, and those two items become even more attractive as things to have.

From the human point of view, we need to keep you safe from a dog that is possessive, and we need to reduce his desire to appropriate things that you value. First of all, if your greyhound takes something that you value, don't try and take it away from him: giving him your attention when he has possession of it is rewarding for him, and you also run the risk of a confrontation. A much better ploy is to distract him by making straight for the treat box calling him excitedly, or by rushing out into the garden with one of his favourite toys. Whatever you choose to do, make it more exciting than what he is doing so that he can't resist. When his attention is distracted, subtly remove the appropriated object, and put it where he can't get to it.

If he is possessive about places such as his bed or the sofa, or even your bed, use distraction again. His own bed is fair enough as a 'no go' area, but if you want to get him off *your* bed be wary of grabbing at his collar, as greyhounds are often sensitive about their necks, and you run the risk of causing him to react defensively. Distract him with a game or treats, or go and get his lead so you can call him off it.

You should also organize things so that any other places he has decided to 'appropriate' will not be available to him in future. So if he has defended your bed, don't allow him in the bedroom; and if he has defended your sofa, either put the cushions up, or throw a few books on it when it is not in use so that he can't use it. If you have made the rule that his bed

is his own private place, it is only fair that he leaves your places alone; however, never send him to his bed as a punishment, but make it a nice place to be. He will soon understand that he must not guard these other places.

In Chapter 5, I wrote about rescue dogs and greyhounds being unaware that food around the house is not for them. If your dog does raid the bin or find something edible out on a walk, he may not like being confronted. Find a better place to keep the bin, where he can't get to it; and if he finds something out on a walk, distract him with a treat, then lead him away from his find.

MOUTHING

Many dogs love to 'mouth' people, ranging from holding a person's hand gently in their mouth, to nipping in excited play. Greyhounds that have not had much opportunity to socialize when young will often do this. As the play becomes more exciting the nips will hurt. So when does it stop being a playful nip and start being a bite?

When puppies play together and when they play with their mother, they will nip each other. If they nip too hard the other puppy or the mother will yelp loudly and then refuse to play any more. This is how a dog learns not to nip too hard. If your dog is a serial mouther, do exactly what a puppy would do: yelp loudly, then turn away and ignore the dog for a few minutes. Do this even when the nip or mouthing doesn't hurt, because if you leave it until the time it really hurts it's a bit too late!

In the past we would have been advised to say 'No' firmly, or we would have got cross when the nip hurt – but by behaving as another dog would, we are

When does playful mouthing stop being play and become a bite?

talking to our dog in his own language. It is much easier for *him* to understand than ourselves.

JUMPING UP

You may like it if your dog jumps up at you when you come in, but your friends may not be too keen on a 30kg (66lb) missile launching itself at them, so this is something you may need to work on. The dog jumps up because he is seeking your attention. If you respond by saying 'No', you are in fact still giving him the attention he is craving, so you have made jumping up worth his while. Rather, when you come in, as soon as your dog goes to jump up, step out of the way so he lands on – nothing. If there is no room

to step away, push him down and turn away. Ignore him until he has all four feet on the floor, and only *then* make a fuss of him, when he is on the floor. If you keep ignoring the bad behaviour and only rewarding the good, he will soon get the message that you will only interact with him when he is *not* jumping up.

Next you need to educate your visitors to do the same. Ask them to ignore him when they enter the house. If they look at the dog and speak to him, he will look on that as an invitation to greet them face to face. If I have someone frail coming I give the dog a toy to play with or a chew bone, and then the problem doesn't arise. For some reason some people think it is a good idea for the visitor to have a titbit to give the dog when they come in, but I don't understand the point of this. All it does is cause the dog to mug visitors for food the minute they enter the house; it doesn't make him like them any more than he likes any other person: he will just regard them as a full dog bowl.

SOUND SENSITIVITY

Many breeds of dog are nervous about strange noises, such as fireworks, for example. Greyhounds have often come from racing kennels which may be in some remote part of Ireland, so they find the sound of heavy traffic, gun shots and fireworks disturbing. The first time they hear these sounds they may cringe and look at you to see what your response is. If you just carry on with whatever you are doing as if nothing is wrong they may well decide 'Right then, that is nothing to be scared of', and you have avoided the problem developing. However, if you try to soothe the dog and sympathize with him he will start to believe there really *is* something to be scared of, and may develop a long-standing fear of the noise.

If your dog already appears to have a fear of certain noises, help him to relax by completely ignoring him. Put some music or the TV on, sit down comfortably, stretch and yawn. After a while he will begin to see that you aren't worried, so there is no need for him to worry. At most pet shops you can buy a CD that has these sounds on it, which you can play softly, increasing the noise level gradually over a few days to acclimatize him.

Remember, if you give sympathy to a dog, it simply feels to him as if you are joining with him in feeling fearful. Therefore resist the temptation to sympathize because you will make things worse.

Some greyhounds may have been trained with livebait, even though this is illegal. A rabbit will scream in fear. A dog that has been trained in this way may respond excitedly and aggressively to screaming sounds, though this is rare. Such a dog will need expert help to desensitize it.

TOUCH SENSITIVITY

Some greyhounds are scared of being touched around their ears or neck; some are funny about their feet. Often when you go to take hold of the collar they will squeal in fear. Spend plenty of time stroking your dog in the areas he is happy with, and occasionally running your hand over the sensitive area until he becomes accustomed to being handled all over. If at any time he becomes suddenly still when you are doing this, remember this is his first way of giving you a warning that he can't cope with it yet, and leave it for another day.

CAR TRAVEL PROBLEMS

It is very rare that retired greyhounds have a problem with car travel. In the past their only outing has been to the races, so most greyhounds are in the car before you have finished opening the door! Very occasionally you might have one that is unhappy about travel and becomes a shivering wreck, in which case arrange for someone to sit with him in the back seat of the car, or to drive while *you* sit with him. Ask them to put their arm across the dog so that he knows they are there, but to offer no sympathy. If the dog gets up to look around during the journey, or makes any interaction with them, ask his companion to reward him with a bright 'Hello boy!'.

Greyhounds love to run, and it is wonderful to see them go.

Keep the journeys short, and build up to longer journeys gradually. It is amazing how well this works. People who have spent years giving their dogs sedatives before shutting them in the dog compartment have been amazed by the improvement in the dog when sitting with a human companion. You can make sure your dog is safe travelling on a seat by using a harness that clips to the seatbelt.

CHASING

Chasing cannot really be classed as a problem because this is what greyhounds do, and it is wonderful to see them run. It isn't really appropriate to be dissatisfied with your greyhound if it sees something small and furry and gives chase. Occasionally I have heard of people resorting to cruel methods to stop a retired greyhound chasing – but if this has worked, it has only been temporary. To change a greyhound that much is like brainwashing. You are trying to change its whole personality. Not only has he got chasing in his genes, but his whole life from a pup

has been directed towards chasing, and indeed doing it to the best of his ability to please his owner and trainer.

Muzzle him to make sure that he cannot harm other people's small furry pets, and give him plenty of 'chase and catch' games in the garden so that his instinctive needs are met. If he ever does get hold of someone's small furry pet he will let go if you lift his back legs off the ground – but greyhounds are so fast that the pet may be fatally wounded already, so use the muzzle to avoid such an occurrence.

THE INDOOR KENNEL

The indoor kennel can be a really useful piece of equipment, but used wrongly it becomes nothing more than a cage. It can be used for the dog when you are concerned about separation anxiety, when you have a small baby visiting and you don't know how good with babies your dog will be, or when you have two dogs in the home who don't know each other well enough to share. However, shutting the door too often and for too long makes it a cage: ideally you should make it into a really cosy den which very occasionally has the door shut.

Set the kennel up in a comfy space, out of the way of human traffic but enough in touch that the dog won't feel excluded. Put his bed in, and a non-spill water bowl (or you can get attachments to hook a bowl on the side of the kennel), and put his toys and chews in it too. Remove other beds so the indoor kennel becomes the most comfortable place to sleep. Keep returning his toys to the kennel. Now he has to go there for comfort, water, toys, in fact everything he values. Make it like a treasure chest.

After a few days he will have decided it is his den, and you will be able to leave him in there for a little while with the door shut. Always coax him in by throwing a treat in so that it is his decision to go in. *Never* send him in as punishment or it will no longer be his 'treasure chest'. If he starts to cry when he is in there, ignore him; open the door when he is quiet.

It is much better if you can plan ahead to make the indoor kennel a nice place to be, but sometimes you have to use one as an emergency, with no practice runs and no chance to set it up as a den. Even so, try to give the dog plenty of safe, interactive toys such as a stuffed rubber toy specially made with a hole that you can fill with food which he can lick out. (Make sure you use a large toy, as dogs have been known to get their tongues stuck in ones that are too small; then the tongue swells, and an emergency visit to the vet is needed.)

THE PICKY FEEDER

Most greyhounds do not over-eat, and will leave their bowl when they have had enough. Like us there are individual metabolisms within the breed, so some will put weight on easily, some have good appetites and the opposite is true. Some dogs are shy about eating when they come to a new home. It is almost unheard of for a dog to starve itself to death. Even Greyfriars Bobby, who was famous for haunting the place where his owner died, accepted food from those who offered it. The more you worry and fuss about your dog's low appetite, the more under pressure he will feel. Providing you know he is not ill, put his food down at the usual time and if he hasn't eaten it in ten minutes, pick it up and take it away. Don't replace it till the next mealtime, even if he has eaten nothing. Keep doing this and eventually he will start eating again.

Never try to coax him by touching the bowl or hand feeding: if you do, he might eat a little but it won't solve the problem in the long run. Often it helps to feed a picky feeder beside another dog, as there is competition for the food – but of course be on hand to make sure the dog who finishes first does not try to get the other dog's food. Trust the dog to know how much he needs to eat (unless he is a glutton). Think what it feels like when you really don't want to eat any more and someone puts pressure on you. If he really doesn't want to eat what you offer, after a few days you could try a different diet – but that may upset him too. You would be better researching a really good diet with less than 20 per cent protein, and sticking to it.

GROWLING AT THE BABY OR TODDLER

When a dog of any breed attacks a baby and has to be euthanased I feel so sad, because this whole situation could, and should have been avoided. A dog that attacks a child attacks because there was nowhere else for him to go. He isn't nasty: he will have given several warnings, but tiny children don't understand these and will invade a dog's space. Just a few plans in place can stop this happening.

Babies crawling towards a dog are very confusing for him. What are they? Are they predatory? Toddlers give dogs the same sort of worry. Are they human? Why do they walk strangely and keep falling over? Babies don't show body language that a dog can read and understand. Many dogs cope brilliantly when the baby becomes more mobile, but some find it very alarming. Usually the dog that finds a crawling baby frightening will find a safe place – a niche, or his bed, or maybe up higher on the sofa. But when the baby is mobile enough to crawl across to where the dog is, the dog will feel the need to defend his safe place, and this is when dreadful things happen with sad outcomes for everyone. Dogs and babies should never be left alone together. Even if you put a training programme in place to help the dog cope with the baby you can never guarantee that the baby will be safe.

A dog and a baby can live together well as long as you put safeguards in place before the child becomes mobile. It is best to let the dog get used to a comfy bed in one room where the baby will never go. Have a stair gate closing this room off so that the dog can still see and hear you but is separated from the baby; it can be a study, a conservatory or a utility room, but it must be a place where the dog will be comfortable. The dog can join you and the baby when you are able to concentrate on them both. Allow the dog to come to the baby, but do not let the baby invade the dog's space. If you need to change your concentration for a second – for example if the doorbell rings – put the dog back in his safe place before you go to the door. Don't take risks. Once you are in the habit of organizing this situation it gets easier. If the dog cries when it is another room, ignore it. Say and do nothing, but go and reward it when it is quiet, so that it understands what you want.

SEEKING HELP

Most retired greyhounds give no trouble at all but just slot into your life as if they have always been there. If you are gentle and consistent with them, they will be gentle and consistent with you. If, however, your dog develops a behaviour that is strange or inconsistent, ask yourself what has changed that may have upset him? Or what is missing from his life that he needs? Dogs don't turn nasty, they just become frustrated about something and don't know how to tell you. If you can't get to the bottom of it, ask your greyhound charity for advice, or seek the help of a professional – but don't blame the dog.

Don't be embarrassed if you have to seek help from a professional behaviourist or trainer if you can't solve the problem. Good greyhound re-homing charities will refer you to one. Seeking further help is a step forwards. No matter how much you know about dogs, new information based on research is coming in all the time. Thinking you know it all, and not seeking help, is a step backwards. When a dog shows undesirable behaviour it will worsen unless you get the right help early on.

10 OBEDIENCE TRAINING

All any dog wants to know when he is interacting with humans is 'What's in it for me?'; once you have recognized this, training becomes easy. First you need to find what your dog's best motivator is: is it a treat, a game with a soft toy, or praise? Often we value praise more than our dog does, so a treat is most likely to work best. Strong-smelling treats such as frankfurter pieces or bits of tripe stick are great, but they make your pockets smell awful. Little pieces of cooked liver work well, too.

So the best answer to 'What's in it for me?' is 'A reward, but only if you do it right; nothing in life is free, from now on every treat has to be earned'. It is a good idea to cut your dog's meal down a little so he is a bit hungry during the weeks that you are working on his training. This way he will not put on too much weight, and he will learn much more quickly because he will be that little bit hungry.

Using rewards is positive reinforcement. There are ways of using negative reinforcement, but the positive works much better. Think of when you were a child in a maths lesson: you do a whole page of work, and it comes back covered in angry red crosses. You lose interest in that work, then you begin to hate the subject, and finally you stop trying. This was negative reinforcement, and it didn't really help you learn.

Now think of the same maths lesson, but this time the teacher comes round and checks how you are doing before you have gone too far. She praises you for the amount you have done, and quietly puts you straight where you are going wrong. Suddenly you feel good because she has praised you for working hard, and you know that with her help you too will get all ticks at the end of the lesson. You feel empowered, and you think she is the best teacher in the world and you would do anything for her. This is positive reinforcement.

Which teacher will best help the child learn? Which teacher would you rather be?

THE RECALL

It is unlikely that your retired greyhound will have learnt recall. Many people take their new dog home and think that he will just become accustomed to his name, and will realize that when you say his name you want him to come. They don't appreciate that they have to teach this, and that the lesson will mean nothing to the dog unless you make it worth his while. It's amazing the number of people who say that their dog won't come to the recall, and when you ask them how long they have spent teaching it they suddenly become very vague.

Let him off the lead in the garden. In kennels he will probably have had time out in an exercise paddock, though when someone came out to collect him he may have realized that that was the end of his moment of freedom and refused to be caught; so now, allow him to mooch around and play with him. When he has realized that coming near you does *not* mean being put on the lead again and taken indoors, it is time to work on the recall. With a titbit ready, wait until he is coming towards you anyway so he can't fail, then call his name and show him the treat, crouching down and making your voice encouraging (you may feel silly, but if you wiggle at the same time, to a dog this is like an invitation to play!). Make yourself the nicest place to be. As soon as he gets to you, give him the treat, and don't then throw it all away by asking for anything more, such as 'sit' or 'paw': just allow him to wander off freely again.

Never try to call him when he is focused on something else, you will simply reinforce failure. Repeat this a few times, then give him a break before trying it again. Keep returning to practise this over the next few days, and avoid calling the dog when you don't have a reward. Even when you have him returning really well, keep practising to reinforce it. Try it in other well fenced, safe places, too. When you are out on walks you can use a long line (not an extending ratchet lead) and practise recall with him still on the lead. Continue with the treat reward system until he is responding automatically. Then you can move on to using praise, or a favourite soft toy to play with instead of a treat sometimes, so that he is never quite sure which result it will be, but it will be a good one – this gives training the excitement of bingo or lucky dip, so that just as the whole idea of coming back for a treat every time was becoming jaded, the dog moves on to thinking 'What will I get? Will it be a treat or…?'

Recall: Alastair crouches down so he doesn't look intimidating.

Recall: he shows Queenie the treat and calls her invitingly.

Recall: when she takes the treat he doesn't spoil it by putting her lead on or asking her to do anything more. Now she knows it is worth coming when he calls.

Never use your dog's name crossly. You will hear people out in the park when their dog doesn't come immediately using an increasingly angry tone. A dog is not going to return willingly to someone who sounds like that, and he will become increasingly dead to his name.

If your dog has been doing something you don't want him to do, or has been slow returning, you should still welcome him like your long lost son once he does return. If you are angry or, worse still, punish him physically, he will be justified in never returning to you again. You wanted him to come and he came eventually, so in the end you did get him to do what you wanted.

Never give chase if he doesn't come because he will think it is a game and will run further and further away – rather, make a noise that catches his attention, and then run *away* from him. He will soon come tearing after you.

If you have a moment when you need to catch a dog that really refuses to come,

get a toy out of your pocket and invite him to play tug of war, or crouch down and investigate something on the floor, or rattle a sweet paper until curiosity brings him back. But this is crisis management for an untrained dog that has slipped its lead, and you should make sure you don't get into this situation in the first place.

THE SIT

Sit? I can hear all experienced greyhound owners saying 'What on earth is "sit" doing here?'. That is because greyhounds do not usually sit. Occasionally you may see one sit for a few seconds, but because of their shape it is an extremely uncomfortable and unnatural position for them. So please do not even think of teaching a greyhound to sit.

WALKING ON THE LEAD

Almost all retired greyhounds, with very

Ex-racing greyhounds have usually been taught to walk calmly on the lead without pulling.

few exceptions, walk beautifully on a slack lead, and never pull! If you get one that does pull, your life will be much easier, and safer, if you spend some time retraining it. I think sight hounds are easier to retrain than scent hounds simply because they naturally walk with their heads up as opposed to walking with their noses on the ground sniffing for a scent.

First, practise in an area where you can keep changing direction. The garden is a good place because the dog will not experience too many distractions on such familiar territory. Have the dog on the lead and keep walking around, every few steps suddenly turning left or right, stopping and starting, and even going backwards so that your dog realizes that unless he pays attention to you he is either going to be trodden on or get left behind. Practise it every day. While you are retraining a dog on the lead, abandon walks: there is no point training him in the garden and then having him haul you off down the street in his usual way afterwards.

Once you feel that the dog is watching where you go and is aware of you as the person who decides where you go, rather than the person he tows along, venture outside the garden. Be prepared that you may not get far. Start walking, and as soon as your dog goes in front, stop. Gently winch him back beside you and set off again. Keep repeating this, and eventually he will realize that he only gets anywhere if he stays beside you. In the first days you may move only a few paces, but the more demanding you are of perfection, the more quickly he will understand; so don't think 'Oh, he is not pulling much so I won't stop yet' because this will just confuse him and delay his learning. There is no point in getting

If a dog pulls, a halti or gentle leader is a helpful aid to stop the walker being pulled over.

cross and hauling him or jerking him back, because he will never want to walk beside you then! It can take weeks of only progressing a few yards to retrain a confirmed puller, but what a wonderful reward it is when you can rely on him to be an absolute star on the lead.

During this time, unless he learns quickly, he may not be getting proper walks so give him plenty of time in the garden.

If your dog really pulls and you haven't got the time or patience to retrain him, use a halti, an easy walker or a gentle leader. This will save you from being towed into dangerous situations. The difference is amazing, and serious pullers will feel like a feather in one of these. If your dog needs to be walked in a muzzle you can still fit a basket muzzle, with an open weave underside, over the halti or gentle leader and thread the part the lead will be attached to through the open weave in the bottom of the muzzle. A harness will not help you with a dog that pulls. The harness is fitted round the chest, and greyhounds have a big, powerful chest; he will be able to tow you along even better in a harness. However, a harness is excellent for a dog that might slip his collar.

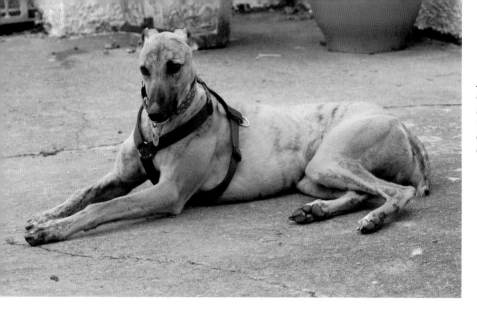

A harness is excellent for a nervous dog that might easily slip its collar.

WALKING TO HEEL

If you want your dog to walk to heel, start at home in the garden. I take advantage of fortunate moments; for example, if my dog is walking beside me of his own accord I pat my leg and say the word 'heel' invitingly, we walk together for a few seconds, and then I stop and reward him. If, when I set off again, he looks like repeating the game, I do it again. When I feel he is developing an understanding, I will invite him to walk with me at my instigation for a few seconds, followed by a treat. I always stop and deliver the reward before he loses interest. If he breaks away first you have blown the opportunity of being the one who is making the decisions. Make the whole thing fun; it should never be a chore.

When you feel he is really grasping the concept, gradually add turns, stops and starts. Keep each session short. Build up to longer distances over time. All this work would be spread over a few days. Like us, dogs seem to learn better when they have a period of rest from training, they seem to come back refreshed and with better understanding almost as if they have had a period of reflection. If your dog knows the treats are in your pocket it does help him to concentrate. Progress to doing a little bit of heelwork when you are walking in a safe place, elsewhere. Choose a time when your dog is not distracted by anything else. Go back to keeping it really short at first and building up the distance. However reliable he becomes at heelwork, never rely on it in public, especially near roads. He is doing it from choice and if he sees a cat the choice will change in less than a second. In public places your dog should be on a lead.

THE LIE DOWN

Well, if we can't do sit, let's try lie down. Normally I would train a dog to move from 'sit' to 'lie down', but this is inappropriate for a greyhound. I work in two ways. First, if I see my dog buckling his legs about to lie down, I take advantage of this and as he does so I say 'Lie down!', and give him a treat when he is down; however this doesn't happen often enough to be more than a back-up to creating a training situation. My second method is to hold a treat that I have let the dog see, in a closed fist, then to crouch down on hands and elbows holding the fist close to my chest; the greyhound will follow the treat with his nose until he is lying down. You can also do this by holding the treat under a chair or low table so that the dog has to crouch down to get to it. Remember to give him the cue 'Lie down' as you get down, and reward him with the treat when he joins you.

I need to warn you that greyhounds take a notoriously long time to learn these things. Whilst a border collie will learn in one or two attempts and then be asking 'What's next, then?', a greyhound is far too laid back to get worked up over anything that isn't to do with chasing, and will take forever to learn the finer points of 'obedience'.

THE STAY

I don't mind whether my dog is sitting or lying when I teach stay, as long as he does stay. If a greyhound is lying comfortably he won't go anywhere anyway, and is

Alastair and Queenie proving that they both know the instruction 'lie down'.

Greyhound demonstrating the stay.

Border collie demonstrating the stay.

I don't expect a greyhound to lie to attention like a border collie when practising the 'stay': it is more likely to settle down for a snooze!

99

more likely to fall asleep, so the 'stay' command is fairly irrelevant. I don't expect my greyhound to lie to attention gazing at my disappearing back ready to spring into action at a signal. It might be achievable, but I am not convinced, and it would take such time and patience to achieve that I don't think the outcome would be worth it. I am happy if they stay in the area that I indicate they should stay in, but I don't expect a statue.

To teach 'stay' I use a gate. I am lucky that I have two parts to my garden with a gate in between, but you can do this in the house using a door – a glass door is best so you can still see each other. As I go through the gate and the greyhound steps forwards to come with me I hold my hand up in a stop sign and say 'Stay'. For the first few times I shut the gate and stay just long enough the other side for the dog to remain in one place watching me to see what I am doing. Then before he loses interest I step back through and reward him. I move on to leaving the gate slightly ajar, though not wide enough for him to get through without pushing. If he steps forwards I step towards him and repeat the word 'stay', and give the stop sign. If he continues to keep coming forwards I know I have moved to the next step too early and need to go back to the previous step a few more times.

Gradually I move on to leaving the gate more open, moving further away, and spending more time at the other side of the gate, remembering only to reward successful cooperation. If the dog blows it at some stage and doesn't stay, I don't get cross, I simply don't reward him, and I take the lesson back a step. This will be done over a few days. Then I incorporate the same training elsewhere. You need to decide what level of cooperation from the dog is acceptable to you. When you increase the period of time your greyhound has to stay, typically he will probably walk a circle and then settle down for a nap – but he has at least stayed where you asked him to, so has he done right or wrong?

As with heelwork, don't even think about asking a greyhound to stay reliably in a public place. First, they are fairly unreliable on this; and second, someone may well kidnap them while you are some distance away, to take home and use for hare coursing.

THE LEAVE

Some greyhounds that have not tested as 'cat friendly' will learn to leave things such as cats alone on command, though they will still go for the cat if you are not there. However the leave command can be useful and I am pleased to say that greyhounds learn this command reasonably quickly. Hold a treat in your open hand, where the dog can see it. As the dog goes to take the treat say 'Leave' firmly and close the hand. Repeat this a few more times. The word 'Leave' must always be loud and firm like a command because the chances are that you might be using this in an emergency one day. When the dog looks at your open hand and doesn't come, or even looks away, go to him and give him the treat.

Keep repeating this game, then move on to dropping the treat on the floor saying 'Leave' and using your other hand in a stop sign. Again once the dog moves away or looks away from the treat, pick up the treat and go and give it to him. Now move on to throwing the treat on the ground some distance away, following the same routine. When you feel you are ready, move on to throwing the treat

A PAT (Pets as Therapy) dog is greeted with delight by the patient he visits.

towards the dog. Try doing this with other items like soft toys, but backstep to dropping the item first and progress from there to throwing again. Remind the dog of this lesson on a regular basis, always backing up with a reward, so that on the day it goes toward something you are really worried about you have an emergency stop procedure in hand.

THE RETRIEVE

I have dealt with this in the chapter on games as it is not a natural greyhound trait; however, it can be used for exercise and stimulation in a retrieve-like game.

TRAINING CLASSES

If you decide to take your retired greyhound to training classes, check first whether the staff have any experience of working with greyhounds. Some trainers find it hard to accept that greyhounds don't sit, that they are indifferent about 'stay', and that they usually need a little snooze half way through the lesson. Think about what you want your greyhound to learn, ask yourself if you have a realistic goal, then explain to your trainer what you want him to help you with. And if you feel he doesn't understand greyhounds, go somewhere else.

Children gain confidence when reading to this greyhound in school.

ADVANCED TRAINING

I haven't included this as a separate chapter because you may have gathered by now that training is not really a greyhound thing. However, because of their wonderfully laid back nature there are fantastic opportunities for them to become an asset to society in a further capacity.

Many greyhounds become PAT dogs (PAT stands for 'Pets as Therapy'). These are dogs that visit people who are in hospital, hospices, residential care homes, day centres and special needs schools. These dogs do not have to train as such but are assessed on their natural temperament and suitability. Retired greyhounds are remarkably good at this work and have brought joy to thousands of sick and old people over the years.

I was recently entertained at a show by a dog from the charity I work for, doing heelwork to music. Although the field of heelwork to music is dominated by such breeds as the border collie, this was really different and enchanting to watch. So greyhounds can be trained to do this. Recently another dog from the charity I work for became a reader's dog, going into schools and listening to the children who have very little confidence while they read from their reading books. Children loved reading to him and he was such a patient listener that the children soon gained in confidence. An adult sat quietly in the background to offer help if the child got stuck. This requires no advanced training, but the dog needs to be assessed to make sure it has the right temperament.

Greyhounds have also qualified as hearing dogs for the deaf. In this case the dog will alert its deaf owner if something is going on that the owner needs to know but can't hear, such as a pot boiling over.

Looking at the streamlined body of a greyhound you might think that they would be good at agility. Certainly this is true of lurchers, some of which are greyhound crosses, but greyhounds seem to be too gangly – they don't crouch naturally, so they don't find the tunnels easy. Also they hate standing on anything moving, so they would probably abandon the seesaw; and although they are fast, they are not in fact very agile compared with lurchers and collies, and of course are far too lazy to take it seriously! However, some have succeeded in this field, though they are not usually fast enough to be winners.

11 RESPONSIBLE GREYHOUND OWNERSHIP

For the safety of your greyhound, and recognizing that greyhounds are hunting dogs, it is wise to spend some time looking at the responsibilities that ownership of a retired greyhound brings. Some of these areas have been visited in previous chapters, but I think it is important to collect them together in one chapter as a reminder for the reader.

IDENTIFICATION

Firstly, remember that your greyhound must wear a collar with an identification tag bearing your name, address and telephone number. This is a legal requirement under The Control of Dogs Order 1992. If your dog does not have a proper identification tag you can be fined up to £5,000.

It is a legal requirement that all dogs must wear an identification tag, even if they are also microchipped.

A soft indoor collar with an identity tag helps to keep your dog safe and comfortable at home.

Although many people like to take their dog's collar off at home, it does make him vulnerable. If he slips past you and off down the road when you open the door, without a collar he has no means of identification. I have soft indoor collars also bearing identity tags for my dogs when they are indoors. They are not strong enough to be used for walking out with dogs that have a strong chase instinct, so I put on leather outdoor collars when we go out. I have heard of so many dogs of all breeds that have been lost by devastated owners who just didn't take that little extra care.

If your greyhound is not yet micro-chipped, neutered and vaccinated you need to arrange this as soon as possible, and keep his vaccinations up to date to protect him from potentially fatal diseases.

INSURANCE

Insurance is not expensive and should also be arranged, preferably before you take your dog home. Some charities will give you a voucher for four weeks free insurance to start you off when you collect the dog. You never know when your dog might become ill and need expensive treatment.

Also if your dog causes an injury or an accident you could be liable for a huge amount of money. We all think we are careful dog owners and it won't happen, but it needs only one caller to leave the gate open. Before the dog even arrives, work with other members of the family at practising shutting doors and gates – you can also fit return springs on them – so that by the time he moves in, everyone is on board about safety. Be aware that a dog that sees a cat in the street can easily squeeze past you at the door if you are not quick enough.

It is illegal and anti-social to allow your dog to foul in a public place unless you clear it up.

CLEAR UP AFTER YOUR DOG!

If you allow your dog to foul in a public place you can be fined £50 on a fixed penalty notice, or you can be taken to court and fined £1,000. I usually carry a pack of nappy sacks in my pocket. Put your hand into a nappy sack and use it like a glove to pick the offensive item up, turning the sack inside out to contain it and knotting it up at the top. Then it is safe to discard in a bin. You can use any plastic bags, but nappy sacks are not see-through and they smell nice, which makes the job a bit more pleasant. All of us hate stepping in dog mess, and leaving it for people to step in gives dog owners a bad name – so please clear up after your dog.

PREDATORY BEHAVIOUR

When you let your greyhound out in the garden off the lead for the first few times, put on his muzzle so that the local cats and wildlife have time to register the fact that a fast dog has moved in. Even if your dog is cat-friendly towards the resident cat, he will regard strange cats in his garden as fair game. If your dog does get hold of a small animal, lift his back legs immediately to make him let go.

If you have small animals such as caged rabbits or guinea pigs, don't allow your dog to terrorize them through the cage wire. Try to keep them well out of his reach, as small animals can easily be literally frightened to death.

When you walk him in a public place, use the muzzle right from the beginning. He has only recently come from the race track, where chasing small furry things with a view to kill was the right thing to do. If people seem frightened by the fact that he is wearing a muzzle, take time to explain that he is not a dangerous dog, but that you are a responsible owner with a rescue dog. Never let children hold the lead until you are sure it is safe for them to do so, and never use an extending ratchet-type lead.

Wait at least two months before you start letting your greyhound off the lead, and use that time to build up perfect recall. When you first let him off the lead, choose a safe, enclosed space, keep his muzzle on, and have ready titbits that you can feed through the muzzle. Even though my greyhounds have excellent recall I always muzzle them when they run loose in case someone's kitten should wander across their path.

Never forget that greyhounds like to hunt and chase. If I let either of my greyhounds play individually in the garden with a friend's Jack Russell there is no problem. If I let them both play with him, the game suddenly turns predatory and becomes 'Get the Jack Russell'! If you have more than one greyhound, please be aware that they may become partners in crime, and egg each other on to predatory behaviour.

BEWARE THEFT!

Never leave a greyhound tied up outside a shop, or unattended in an accessible garden. These dogs are highly prized and frequently stolen for illegal racing, or dog-napped for a ransom. This sounds melodramatic, but it is true. In my area last year four dogs were dog-napped and sold back to their owners for three-figure ransoms by people who pretended to have rescued them.

If you should lose your dog, at the end of this book there are details of a website that you can use to help you set up a nationwide hunt almost immediately.

The more quickly you use this, the greater the chance you have of retrieving your dog. Lost dogs that are picked up by the dog warden are usually taken to a dog pound miles away, and it is up to you to contact the dog warden and track down your dog. The police are often far too busy to deal with lost dogs. If the dog has been stolen, nationwide awareness makes it too hot to handle for the thief and they will often abandon the dog where you can find it, or find a way of handing it back.

CHECKLIST

The following is the responsible greyhound owner's checklist:

- Identification
- Micro-chipping
- Dog-poo bags
- Neutering
- Vaccinations
- Insurance
- Closing doors and gates
- Muzzle
- Off-lead safety
- Greyhounds as predators
- Dog theft
- Dog loss

AND FINALLY...

If you are a greyhound owner I hope this book has helped you to understand your dog better, and that you have become more aware of what his life may have been like before he was ready to hang up his racing colours and come to you. If you are just about to adopt your new greyhound I hope it will help you in helping your dog make an easy transition from race track to home. Enjoy your greyhound: he will be your friend for life.

APPENDIX 1: FOREVER HOUNDS TRUST

Forever Hounds Trust is the leading independent greyhound rescue charity in England and Wales, dedicated to the rescue, rehabilitation and re-homing of abused and abandoned greyhounds and greyhound crosses. Formed in 1991, it became a registered charity five years later. The charity now re-homes almost 600 of these special dogs every year.

Forever Hounds Trust's main areas of operation are Hertfordshire, Worcestershire, Herefordshire, Gloucestershire, Shropshire, Cheshire, Lancashire, Somerset, Dorset, Devon and Cornwall, and with representation as far east as Buckinghamshire, Bedfordshire and Hampshire. The charity is completely staffed by volunteers across these areas.

Forever Hounds Trust takes in greyhounds and greyhound crosses from members of the public, veterinary surgeries, dog wardens and the police. We also help trainers and owners re-home their racing greyhounds, and dogs also come to us from general rescue centres. Some greyhounds come from as far afield as Wales, Scotland and Ireland if resources allow.

On entry to the charity every dog is neutered, vaccinated, micro-chipped and vet-checked before it is homed. In kennels the dog will be cat-tested and assessed to identify its needs and what type of home it would best suit.

Potential adopters are home-checked before being invited to kennels or foster homes to meet suitable dogs. The home-check procedure is individual to every case; we do not have hard and fast rules that eliminate possible adopters without consideration.

After a dog has been adopted, its new owners receive a follow-up phone call within twenty-four hours, and will be revisited by the home checker after four months. New owners can, at any stage, receive free help from the post-homing support team, a group of volunteers with well recognized behaviour training and qualifications, and experienced with sight hounds.

If you would like a greyhound but your circumstances do not allow you to have one, you can support the 'sponsor a dog' scheme for those dogs that are too damaged mentally or physically to re-home.

Forever Hounds Trust runs a calendar of events where greyhound lovers can meet. You can download membership forms, 'sponsor a dog' forms, and find out about homing a greyhound or volunteering to help the charity by visiting the website www.foreverhoundstrust.org.

APPENDIX 2: UNDERSTANDING A DOG'S RACING HISTORY

An example from the racing career of my dog Safe Flight.

Column one: the date of the race.

Column two: the place (Monmore is an Irish track).

Column three: the distance of the race in metres, then yards; this shows you that Safe Flight was a middle-distance runner.

Column four: the grade. Safe Flight was racing at Grades A7 and A8; she raced at grades A6, A7 and A8 all her racing life so

was never going to be a top dog, which is probably why she was retired at the age of three.

Column five: the number of dogs in the race; it is usually six. On 7 February there was only one dog, because it wasn't a race but a trial, so she ran alone.

Column six: the trap used at the start. In the races Safe Flight started from trap four or five, which tells us she tended to run wide. Trap three would be used on the trial, as there were no other dogs she could run in front of and hamper.

1	2	3	4	5	6	7	8	9
Date	**Stadium**	**Dist M/Y**	**Grade**	**Dogs**	**Trap**	**Stime**	**Posts**	**Fin**
20 Feb 2006	Monmore	480/525	A8	6D	T5	4.52	5553	1st
18 Feb 2006	Monmore	480/525	A8	6D	T4	4.63	5444	5th
7 Feb 2006	Monmore	480/525	Trial	1D	T3			
3 Feb 2006	Monmore	480/525	A8	6D	T5	4.56	6666	6th
30 Jan 2006	Monmore	480/525	A7	6D	T5	4.59	3543	6th

An example from the racing career of my dog, Safe Flight.

Column seven: the time it took for the dog to get from the traps to the winning line on the first circuit; this is called the 'sectional time'.

Column eight: the position this dog was in during the race, at every bend in the race (but only for the first four bends in six- and eight-bend races).

Column nine: the final position. Safe Flight won on 20 February.

Column ten: the grader's thoughts on how the dog ran and what happened to it during the race.

Column eleven: only applicable in open or feature races; it details the points earned.

Column twelve: the bookmakers' odds at the start of the race when the hare starts to run and the book is closed.

Column thirteen: the weight of the dog before the race.

Column fourteen: the name of the winning dog.

Column fifteen: the time recorded for the winning dog.

Column sixteen: how long your own dog took to run the distance.

Column seventeen: the estimated time for the race after any going allowance has been given (for example, is the track soft or hard?).

Column eighteen: the dog's form – as in horse racing, this is between 1–100.

Column nineteen: used to record what film the race can be located on, so it can be watched on Windows media player.

10	11	12	13	14	15	16	17	18	19
Comment	Pts	Sp	Kg	Winner	Win	Time time	Etime	Form	Film
Crowded1 Led Near Line		6/1		Safe Flight	29.55	29.55	29.75	41	
Every Chance		8/1		Rockery Patch	29.42	30.08	30.08	24	
Mid-W									
S. away, crowded		5/1		Fayes Lochron	29.59	30.27	30.17	20	
Every Chance		5/1		Ballydaniel Fozz	29.66	30.10	30.10	23	

FURTHER INFORMATION

FURTHER READING

Understanding the Rescue Dog; all you need to know about re-homing a dog with a past. By Carol Price.

The Culture Clash by Jean Donaldson.

RECOMMENDED GREYHOUND RESCUE CHARITIES

Forever Hounds Trust
www.foreverhoundstrust.org
03000 111 100

Orchard Greyhound Sanctuary
www.orchardgreyhoundsanctuary.com
(Ireland)

Kerry Greyhound Connection
www.kerrygreyhounds.co.uk
07500 062 648 (Ireland)

The Greyhound Sanctuary
www.thegreyhoundsanctuary.org
01865 601 190 (Devon)

Give a Greyhound a Home
www.gagah.co.uk 01224 782 489
(Scotland)

GALA (Greyhound and Lurcher Aid)

Fen Bank Greyhound Sanctuary
www.fenbankgreyhounds.co.uk
01754 820 593 (Lincolnshire)

Black Beauties (this is a website which gathers black dogs of all breeds from various different rescues and has many greyhounds on it)
www.blackbeauties.org.uk

Oldies Club (homes older dogs of various breeds including greyhounds)
www.oldies.org.uk

Greyhound Gap
www.greyhoundgap.org.uk
01782 544 728

Greyhounds Galore
www.greyhoundsgalore.org.uk
01642 322 239 (North East England)

USEFUL WEBSITES

To help find a lost dog
Dog Lost www.doglost.co.uk
0844 800 3220

Forums
Sight Hounds on Line
www.sighthoundsonline.co.uk

INDEX

Page numbers in bold type indicate photographs.